1001

COINCIDENCES

that are not
Coincidences

by TS Caladan

Edited by TS Caladan

Cover Design by TS Caladan

Front Cover Image by Michal Steflovic

Published by TWB Press, https://www.twbpress.com

ISBN: 978-1-959768-57-9

Contents:

Introduction:
An Outsider Interviews an Insider

I want to tell the true story of how this ancient mystery researcher/writer, once met and interviewed Jordan Maxwell in 2004. I was in the Atlantis Bookstore on Burbank Boulevard in LA and viewed a video that the store sold. I was instantly intrigued by it. Not because of its production quality (very poor quality and only a few people in his audience as he lectured), but by what the disk told me. Information about the masons or Illuminati that I had never heard before. Who was Jordan Maxwell (1940-2022)? "His work uncovering the hidden foundations of Western religions and secret societies creates enthusiastic responses from audiences around the world. His research on the subject of secret societies, both ancient and modern, and their symbols, has fascinated crowds from many countries for 4 decades."

The disk I viewed informed me what the mysterious letters and symbols on our dollar bill really meant. Other symbols and emblems that we outsiders never knew and took for granted, suddenly were revealed and it was *fascinating!* The more I watched, the more I learned of Illuminati secrets from a man that studied them for most of his life. But all was not as it seems.

Through the store, I was able to meet the man and he agreed to an interview, which has been posted for 20 years. Myself and a friend met Jordan at a restaurant on Ventura Boulevard. While setting up the meeting; he said: "I don't want to talk about government conspiracies." I was stunned on the other end of the phone. My thought was: *What the hell are we going to talk about, then?* Instead of an evening that I thought might be a bust, it turned out to be a marvelous talk. Pretend you were at the table and listened-in on our conversation. The following is an edited transcript of that meeting:

JM: ...the government doesn't consider you a threat as long as you're just talking. I'm just talking. Not causing violence. And they told me: you don't have much of a following. [laugh] If you start getting a LARGE following like Martin Luther King and you start talking too much, then they are going to deal with you...I have always been fascinated with the world of the Occult. When I say 'Occult,' I'm using it in its classical meaning. It means HIDDEN...

DY: Hidden?

JM: Doesn't mean evil or bad or corrupt. It just means hidden. Secrets. In the medical field, there are terms that doctors use; certain organs are occult, it means hidden or not in view. (Also in astronomy: when a celestial body is behind another, it's occulted).

DY: What of the Roswell aliens? Do you believe William Cooper's book where he states there's a pact between us and the (gray) aliens? We will take technology from them and then cover up their existence?"

JM: I'm just giving you a subjective opinion based on my feelings and talking to people for 40 years on the subject. I am totally convinced something very legitimate happened at Roswell. And I shouldn't be a bit surprised if there were alien bodies there...Plenty of people are giving great documentary proof. But, it doesn't matter how much proof you offer. If people don't want to believe, they're not going to believe even if you saw an alien sitting here...

DY: Might be.

JM: The point being...I believe, without any doubt, that there is, in point of fact, extraterrestrial/alien life here on Earth. I am not sure where they've come from. They may even be indigenous to this planet for billions of years and we're just the newcomers who are now spotting them for the first time...There are many dimensions, they could be with us right here and we don't see them.

DY: I'm convinced there are secret bases on the Moon and Mars. I think they sent 'Spirit' to the Gustav Crater because they knew nothing was in the Gustav Crater. Why aren't they publicly checking the Martian FACE and the pyramids at Cydonia?

JM: I sat for 3 days and 3 nights with Richard Hoagland up in Oakland at a private conclave with 6 other people. Richard Hoagland gave us some really startling information, being a spokesman for NASA. It blew my mind what he was talking about. He did not mention, at all, Mars. He had extensive comments about what NASA knows is going on on the Moon. The Moon is, most likely, hollow. It has a metal superstructure and was probably *brought* here.

DY: Are you a believer in reincarnation?

JM: Yes. I'm totally convinced of that for myself. I have reasons for saying that. I have heard all the other arguments, which are saying that the phenomena that we call Reincarnation is explainable in another way. I still don't buy it.

DY: 1776, the founding fathers were freemasons?

JM: Not all, but yeah.

DY: Was the government originally a good thing, corrupted by the Illuminati over time?

JM: My honest answer is I don't know. I am aware that this country was founded as a corporation. The British East

India Company, which was supposed to be the British East India Tea Company. The British East India Company is involved with the founding of the *corporation called America,* the United States. And when the first 13 colonies were founded, they were not called colonies. In point of fact, they were called 13 individual 'companies.'

DY: Really?

JM: Later on, they became known as the colonies. They were first called 'companies.'

DY: That fits with the Corporation idea.

JM: The Queen of England set up corporations: the East India Company and set up companies around the world...The Vatican is the brains behind the British Empire. It breaks off and becomes another company, but the money is still...you got General Motors and then you have a big fight, a big argument and they set up a new company called Pontiac. Pontiac is still General Motors.

DY: You taught me about the Scottish Rite and York Rite freemasons. Pope, the head of the Church and the Throne of England the head of the State?

JM: When you get into Masonry, you're getting into what I would call a briar patch. There is so much we don't know; there is so much we are not privileged to know. **One thing I am convinced of, beyond a shadow of a doubt, is that everything is connected**. Nobody is an enemy. Nobody is a friend. It's all just business. You will find Scottish Rite masons who are at war with Scottish Rite masons. York Rite masons are at war with somebody else. The Vatican is in it. After awhile, you begin to see everybody is trading their money, trading their stocks.

DY: These are power-plays?

JM: Yeah. That makes sense because one of the most powerful symbols in Freemasonry is 'Ordo Ab Chao,' which is Order Out of Chaos. The idea is: If everything just sits quiet, nothing gets done. The more chaos and all the trouble going on in the world, *stuff gets done!* You can set up police departments, you can set up governments. You can set up an army, have a bigger army. It's all business, don't worry about it.

DY: I sent you that quote from '1984': The war with East-Asia or Eur-Asia did not matter. The war was meant to be continuous. The Ruling Group makes war upon its own subjects...

JM: So they can keep control over you...

DY: And to keep the structure of their Hierarchy intact...Can you tell us anything about this ritual of Killing the King? How the King is not the highest card in the deck: A secret Ace that controls all the Kings?

JM: Yeah. I've studied that subject for 40 years. The whole concept of Jesus, King of Kings, Lord of Lords. He was killed, huh?

DY: I didn't think of that.

JM: And when the King or Queen of England dies, people say: 'The King is dead. The King is dead. Long live the King.' What are you talking about, you just said he was dead? It's part of a ritual. You kill the King because the blood of the King is the resurrection into a newer and higher order...

DY: How did you learn about it?

JM:...There's all kinds of stuff going on, all kinds of levels of symbolism. Occult terms and emblems that are used around the world that most people even in the government today don't know why they got the symbols that they do. They'll sing the Star Spangled Banner. A 'banner' is a word which is used in the corporate world to advertise a company. There is a world of difference between a banner and a flag. If you research this difference, then you're starting to get where I've been for years: looking at the Darkside, the Occult world of words, terms, phrases...

DY: And also colors? You mentioned colors?

JM: Very interesting. Surrender means you have no color. You wave the white flag. If someone blows up at you and you say wow they're showing their true colors. That's what the gangs do, they wear blue, you got a problem with that? And the other gang comes in wearing their red.

DY: If it was a fertilizer bomb in Oklahoma, there would have been a yellow cloud of poisonous ammonia. There was no cloud. To me, it was a sophisticated CIA bomb...

JM: Anybody who can look at the Oklahoma explosion and not see something wrong with it, I don't want to talk to them. It's like what Dick Gregory said: If you know, you know. And if by now, you're so damn stupid that you don't know, you don't deserve to be told. (ha, ha) You're going to blow up a 25-story building with cow poopoo? Seriously?

DY: Do you think it wasn't a coincidence that the high school shooting at Columbine is so close to the name 'Columbia'? [D.C., CBS, Columbia Shuttle disaster, etc.].

JM: Yeah, well. I wouldn't be surprised. Who knows? All I know is that *nothing happens in this world by chance*. That's if something happens, you can damn well figure that somebody planned it that way.

DY: You said Catholicism and Judaism are basically the same in the same way that the throne of England and the Vatican are the same?

JM: Yeah, that's right. It's all just business. Don't take

any of this personal; it's just business.

DY: That round building you said was in Switzerland, divided into thirds: Masons, World Bank and U.N. Is there a name for the building? [The round peace symbol comes from an aerial view of the building with the masons divided into 2 sections. Also seen in the Mercedes-Benz logo].

JM: I found that in 1980, in a World Book Encyclopedia. It was in Switzerland or possibly Belgium.

DY: So, they control the problem and they control the solution?

JM: We've known that for years. Everybody knows that.

DY: I was part of the Peace Movement...and to hear that the people on the top were controlled by the other side?

JM: And that surprises you?

DY: Ha. Winston Churchill with his **'V' for Victory** hand sign. He was a warlock in league with Aleistor Crowley?

JM: Aleistor Crowley came up with that victory-sign, but it wasn't for Victory. (Hippie peace hand sign). It meant something to Aleistor Crowley. It had nothing to do with Victory at all.

DY: Devil worship? Sex?

JM: Whatever it was, it was recommended by Aleistor Crowley to Churchill. **Aleistor Crowley also recommended to Adolph Hitler the stretched out, right-hand salute**...

DY: Really?!

JM: That was Crowley's recommendation to Hitler when he was first coming into power. Incidentally, according to reference works that I've read, the **thumbs up**, that the American soldiers always gave was also from Crowley. He was an extremely respected Occultist, around the world.

<<*Time out! Let's review. You know that THUMBS UP

hand sign that you all do because all movies, sports, animation and tons of other things do it and they've made you accept it as the new Okay sign? It was created by the same evil man that controlled Hitler, Churchill, FDR, Stalin, Tojo, etc. Same guy gave WW2 American pilots that thumbs up sign: "Plane's ready to go!" And the same guy originated the 2-fingered, hippie hand sign (we thought we'd win the social war like the Allies won WW2) that the youth flashed in the sixties. Now to discover that <u>everything is connected</u> and you guys are flashing something very evil today and you don't even know>>.

DY: Was the attack on Pearl Harbor planned? Was FDR in on it? See, I could never tell my father that. The idea was our top military leaders allowed the Japanese attack to happen to bring us into Britain's war?

JM: There is a book written by a man named Colonel Curtis Dall. He was Roosevelt's son-in-law. The book is called 'My Exploited Father In-law.' In that book, he said that Roosevelt had the Act of War on his desk 6 months before it happened.

DY: Before Pearl Harbor?

JM: Of course. It had already been planned.

DY: Just before 9/11, they came out with the movie 'Pearl Harbor.' Why come out with a terrible movie at that time? Also, there were a number of war films then like 'Band of Brothers.' Made to sway us to fear and go to war?

JM: How about 'Wag the Dog'?

DY: Yes. The 10% controlling the 90%.

JM: That's telling you something.

DY: People view it as entertainment, when it's actually brainwashing. Celebrities in the Bohemian Grove: They're told what films they'll be in, who they have to marry or break-up with. Agents and handlers ruling celebrity lives or they will break you...

JM: When you're talking Bohemian Grove, the word 'grove' is code and very important. Look up the word *grove.*

DY: I see a group of robed (pagan) figures out in a grove.

JM: Now, you're getting it.

DY: What about the film 'Eyes Wide Shut'?

JM: That's how most people go through the world, with their Eyes Wide Shut or being blind with open eyes.

DY: I meant how Tom Cruise found himself in a place he shouldn't have been, a place of secret rituals?

JM: Look what happened to Stanley Kubrick – died during the making of the film.

DY: You don't think that just happened?

JM: Look at the subject of the film.

DY: The film did get made.

JM: But, who's to say what it would have looked like if Kubrick had been alive to finish it?

DY: Going back to spending all that time with Richard Hoagland, he didn't mention Mars? I thought that was his specialty.

DY: He might have mentioned Mars. It was 1995. At that time, his interest was not so much Mars as on the Moon. We also spoke about Egypt and some on Cydonia, but not so much about the Face. There was a bit on artificial structures. How pyramids were laid out, and the Sphinx.

DY: William Cooper, who wrote 'Behold a Pale Horse,' do you think he was murdered because of what he knew about the government?

JM: I couldn't testify to anything. I knew Bill Cooper. He had a bad temper. I have a 'suspicion.'

DY: Why was Princess Diana killed?

JM: I sure don't know. My OPINION is Princess Diana was probably far more the legitimate Royalty than who we call the Royalty today. The Royalty, or BRIT-ish, are Saxon: they are German, not English...The Germans wanted to legitimize their English Throne. They wanted Di to marry Charles to add a truly *English* person to their German bloodlines. But, Di was not impressed with the German Royalty that ran everything and she went against them. I don't doubt it.

DY: The Queen Mother is German?

JM: Yes, sure.

DY: When did this German take over of Britain happen?

JM: During the Middle Ages, the coming of the Saxon bloodlines into England. Their banking systems...

DY: Wait, what does that do to WW2?

JM: And World War One.

DY: Yes, also German. England was the vanguard of the war against Germany. Were they fighting themselves?

JM: That's a good question. Politics on a very high level. All I know is: All of the Royal Family are German; there's no English blood.

DY: Diana fulfilled her purpose by producing the children?

JM: Sure. Her brother gave the eulogy at the Church the day she was buried, and said: "Diana's bloodline will protect her two sons."

DY: Thank you, Jordan. It's been a pleasure.

JM: Thank you.

I later asked him: Is there any hope for us on Earth?

According to Jordan, the answer is NO! It's far too late. Humans have lost the war a long time ago. People are far too blind. Ignorance is bliss; the general public doesn't have a clue and will refuse to see the light. The answers, the symbols with their secret meanings, are right in front of us. Fascism is rubbed into our face with symbols, TV brainwashing, corporate logos and federal emblems. There's nothing we can do, not even in the near future, the enemy is too great. The Evil Empire is too large of a monster. I can certainly understand Jordan's utter discouragement and contempt for the walking blind. [Today's term = 'Walking Dead'].

Yes, talking with this Insider I learned a lot. But I soon discovered the truth behind Jordan Maxwell. I found out he was not an angry Conspiracy Theorist who raged against the fascists that ruthlessly ruled our world. He wasn't out to expose the Monarchy and their dirty dealings like I thought he was. Hell, no. He wasn't pissed at THEM...*he was pissed at us!* He was angry at the masses for being so stupid and allowing a fascist state to happen all around us. We completely diverged on this point and I realized: *He was one of them,* a real Insider. That's why he knew so much about Them. He was allowed to expose what he has exposed. That very first disk I saw of him...he spoke of Hegelian Dialectics and it means, basically: a controlled opposition. You send a spy to your enemy's camp. Soon, your man rises up the ranks, takes charge and suddenly: you have no enemy. In time, I learned a good lesson – know your enemy. I thought this might be an appropriate introduction for what is presented in the next pages to come...

TS Caladan

Coincidences that are not

1 MTV just happens to have its New York headquarters inside a Masonic temple. Since music videos were always planned to soon disappear from the television channel...we are left with the conclusion that the channel was always named 'Masonic TV.'

2 New York City, named after British royal bloodlines of the Yorks [They were the Starks in 'Game of Thrones']. Wouldn't early Americans after a Revolutionary War rename the first settlements and distance themselves from anything British? Look how many states, cities and towns remain English in name. This is because the United Kingdom still rules over us in all of our smaller (not sovereign) kingdoms through freemasonry or secret societies. *Who closed the whole planet, mandated masks and had us 6 feet away from each other in one day?* Britain, the only Superpower. "Hey ref, call the play!" "No, we have to hear from New York first."

3 Why does the state flag for Hawaii have a British Union Jack flag in its upper left corner? An oddity, when you discover that England has never owned Hawaii. From the record: The state flag represented "...the Kingdom of Hawai'i, then the Hawaiian Territory, and later the Republic. Today it also represents the Hawaiian sovereignty movement..." The record explains that the flag was determined by close relations between a native ruler and British captains. *I don't buy it. The flag might symbolize that the Sun still never sets on the English Empire.*

4 Is it a coincidence that PURPLE is not allowed on any country's flag and purple is a royal color? If countries were truly sovereign, wouldn't you think one would add purple?

5 American children and junior high students in the '50s and '60s were *forced* to face the flag, place their hand on their heart and recite the Pledge of Allegiance. Every day of school. We did not know what it was they made us say and what they were really doing; we merely followed orders as unsuspecting kids. It is not a coincidence that a nasty, ugly, non-American word like "Republic" was used in our solemn pledge. Note: "I pledge allegiance to the Flag of the United States of America, and to the Republic for which it stands..." The first part is fine: the "U.S." means the land and blue skies. But the word "REPUBLIC" means a "rule by council." **Not a Democracy**! (Look it up). A secret/connected group rules every country, actually. The lie is that we live in a Free World. From the very start, they had us pledging loyalty to a secret totalitarian state. The exact opposite of what a Democracy is supposed to be.

6 Coincidence that the Architects of the planet and the creators of chaos that have placed FEAR into our brains and our souls, had the nerve to call themselves "GREAT Britain"? What other country has a glorious adjective in their title that proudly boasts of their superiority? It is a way of programming people, making them think *Brits are special.* Every time "Great Britain" is said, it's a subliminal message that tells us a lie. The Royals (not the people) are the orchestrators of all wars and they are the Money-Printers that enslave all of you dystopians, who are happy and "empowered" and **Not See** your own imprisonment. Sad. Why does England have the greatest actors, greatest explorers, greatest writers of literature, the greatest music, the

greatest in just about all of the arts and accomplishments? Because they control all means of Media and they TELL US SO.

7 What is the Goat? Everything has turned around, changed upside-down and been inverted. The "goat" was the guy who dropped the ball and lost the game. And nobody wanted to be the hideous *goat* (or scapegoat), as the word was used long ago. But today, G.O.A.T. means the greatest of all time! Sports pundits argue all the time about: Who is the GOAT? A complete reversal from what it was. An ironic coincidence? Not at all, it was planned.

8 Is it a coincidence that old witchcraft books have a GOAT-symbol on their covers within a circle? A 5-POINTED STAR, POINT DOWN, REFERS TO A GOAT: horns, ears and billie-goat beard. We have 50 of them on our flag if you turn it upside-down.

9 Is it a coincidence that Washington D.C. is laid out in a 5-pointed star, easily seen from the air? The famous monuments just happen to be placed at each point? The inner pentagram/Pentagon.

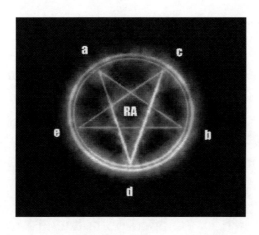

10 The magic phrase of "Abracadabra" originated from the mystical star within a magic circle. Now look at how 5-pointed stars are used in Media, in movies, on TV, in celebrations, on posters and just about everywhere around us. Why not 6 or 7-pointed stars? Nope, it's always 5. And the funny thing is they are usually placed, like product-placements, POINT DOWN! If point-up, the image represents something special and grand, then what's point down mean? Something terrible. Now, you know why the Media uses more goats than it should. The stars refer to the billy goat, which is a satanic symbol. As in the Stones' 'Goats Head Soup' album.

11 Of all the animals the Beach Boys could have used for the cover of their great album 'Pet Sounds,' what did they choose? [Chosen for them, they had no choice]. GOATS. C'mon, people. What do Heavy Metal rockers do (made to do): Flash the hand sign of the Devil. The 'mano cornuto' (horned hand in Italian) *"Rock 'n roll!"*

12 "Kids." Why do we call our children *kids?* We say this because *everyone says it. Everyone's made to say the term.* It's a goat-reference and it's wrong. They should be called "children," not "kids."

13 The similarity between *cattle* and "chattel." Chattel's definition is an item of property other than real estate. Both words have been used to refer to people that are enslaved, owned by the elite Slave-Masters. *We are told what They do.*

14 The members of the Illuminati honor Light and Truth? No, Darkness and Lies.

15 Is it a coincidence that Barack Obama's middle name is 'Hussein,' which just happens to be the last name of Saddam

Hussein? Saddam was president and PM of Iraq for decades. Hussein was found guilty of numerous human rights violations and the disappearance of a few hundred thousand people. He was executed (hung) for crimes against humanity in 2006.

16 Coincidence that the children of President Barack Obama and Michele Obama do not look like the Obamas, and instead, resemble the male and female nannies that always cared for them?

17 LeBron James. Seriously. His name is Le Brawn, which translates to: *the Strong,* and he just happens to have scored the most points in all of NBA history? C'mon. His parents knew? What if they named him: "LeSkinny"? I don't think LeSkinny James would even make the NBA.

18 Now, what do we discover is the name of his supposed son? Is there even a resemblance? His son's name is "Bronny." *C'mon!* No way. Yes way, it's his name...but, he also just happens to be a big, strong guy and will play pro basketball for the Lakers, *his dad's team.* What if Bronny James was not athletically inclined? What if he was a brainy chess-player instead? Brainy James? I guess that wasn't going to happen. *Something's going on.*

19 Wilt "the stilt" Chamberlain was one of the greatest basketball players of all time and still holds numerous records that may never be broken. In his infamous book, the man claims to have *slept with more than 20,000 women!* Wow. You really think that's true? Well, he was a big guy, a very famous man at the time. Something tells me the nickname of "stilt" was a campaign that was untrue. Maybe the "wilt" part is more real and this was another case of over-compensating the truth?

20 Nick Kyrgios is an Australian professional tennis player more famous for his emotional outbursts and crazy antics than his accomplishments on the tennis court. He's today's version of John McEnroe. His name is pronounced "Curious." And Nick sure is a mysterious wonder and a big curiosity, a very talented player that has not lived up to his potential.

21 Usain Bolt. Possibly the fastest runner that's ever been: Is a little insane, but isn't it strange that his last name is 'Bolt'? As in a lightning bolt?

22 Greg Louganis. The diver won gold medals at the '84 and '88 Summer Olympics on the springboard and platform. He has been called: "probably the greatest diver in history." Louganis is a gay rights activist and an advocate for HIV awareness. Is it a coincidence or something else that "gayness" is how one says the last part of his last name?

23 The Olympics have accepted transgender athletes where a man can compete as a woman, under certain conditions. Odd, isn't it? What if this transgender-acceptance is way more prevalent than the general public thinks? Is it a coincidence that every "female" Olympic competitor has a bra-size that is an A-Cup? Couldn't there be one, just one or two that had them floppin' in the wind? Nope, not one.

24 The Disney Corporation is not the "Wonderful World" that we were programmed to think as children. Disney has come under fire for many reasons, one being the inclusion of subliminal sex, from (quick) nudity to Jessica Rabbit's bush, even the word "sex" and many more erotic things not noticed at first glance.

25 Is it a coincidence that 666 or 3 6s are seen in Walt

Disney's signature logo? A signature that was not his actual signature, but one created for the company.

26 Look at the old "Okay" sign we all made of fingers up and thumb that touched the index finger. The hand sign forms 666.

27 Why play sets in tennis to 6? Why not play to 5 or 7? The reason is: At Wimbledon and other major tournaments that play best of 5 sets, quite often, 666 is aligned on the scoreboard.

28 If Disneyland is known for being 'The Happiest Place on Earth,' then why is it also known for having a high number of *suicides* that have happened on its grounds? One theory could be that damn song: 'It's a Small World.'

29 The new Pepsi logo with curved, sweeping lines. Take a closer look at it. The red/blue and white within a circle happens to appear like a snake-eye. This is not a coincidence.

30 Now, look at the image of the bell in Taco Bell ads. The clapper just below the bell is also a snake-eye.

31 In R.J. Reynolds Tobacco Company ads or Joe Camel ads, *Joe's a penis!* This is very well-known.

32 Secret meanings behind Olympic logos through the years. Many of the logos, when switched around, reveal secret messages. Would the Rulers of the World do that? Yes, that's what they do. Hide their pushed Agenda 'In Plain Sight.' There were many articles on the Internet and YouTubes that moved elements of the logos around and showed you what they really meant. Today, those articles and YTs are difficult to find. Now, when the subject is researched, ridiculous and easy to refute explanations are in place, which are pure diversionary tactics. If

there was nothing to the hidden meanings of Olympic logos, then why did Iran threaten to boycott the 2012 Olympic games in London because the logo, when moved around, obviously spelled out "Zion"? A reference to Jewish superiority that offended those from Iran. And also spelled out...

33 Why is it that the members of the so-called *Woke* Movement are actually "Sound Asleep" politically and blinded to what is really going on in the world today?

34 Why is a FASCIST Symbol ("fasces") of tied rods or twigs and an axehead found in America, *the Land of the Free?* The evil symbol goes back to the Roman era. It means: We have power (axe) if we control the leaders (tied rods). What was depicted on the back of the old Mercury dime? A fasces. What are the large emblems hung prominently on the walls in the U.S. House of Representatives, behind the speakers' podium? Two fasces. What is seen on the round seal of the U.S. Senate? Crossed fasces. The image was in newspapers, especially during political campaigns. The fasces was on American newspapers' front page logos, until they were removed long ago. Now, you wouldn't think American institutions would represent a symbol of fascism, but they do.

35 Nazi. Surprise...'Nazi' does not mean 'National

Socialists' like we have been told by Media. The term is derived from the English language. *It's English* and means to NOT SEE. We do not see that we remain under the boots of Big Brother and *men* in High Castles/capstones.

36 Lights went out at Super Bowl 47 in New Orleans between the San Francisco 49ers and the Baltimore Ravens. For 34 minutes the game was halted because of the black-out and the score was: 28 to 7 in favor of the Ravens. Former Raven, Ray Lewis, will tell you who was to blame: "You're a zillion-dollar company, and your lights go out? No. (laughs) No way." He blamed someone who wanted the 49ers to win and they almost did, but came up short on the final drive. Coincidence that SF nearly won after Lights Out?

37 The 27 Club. It is somewhat of an urban legend, but is more than likely true. Famous singers and a few periphery celebrities have died under strange circumstances at the young age of 27. Is it a curse? Were some of them murdered, then the public is given any story they've concocted? A "Hollywood Hit Squad"? Were some of the young stars contracted to receive fame and fortune, but then must "pay the piper" at the age of 27? What really goes on behind the curtains of Hollywood and the Music Industry? The following list of Club members are odd to say the least and cannot be brushed off easily.

38 Brian Jones.

39 Jimi Hendrix.

40 Janis Joplin.

41 Jim Morrison.

42 Kurt Cobain.

43 Amy Winehouse.

44 Jean Michael Basquiat.

45 Anton Yelchin. The last two on the list, painter and actor, are also considered Club 27 members because of their unusual deaths.

46 Anton Yelchin played Chekov in the first remakes of the Star Trek movies. But earlier in 2009, he played Kyle Reese in *Terminator Salvation*. And in the story: The Machines were out to kill Kyle Reese. His bizarre death occurred when his Jeep Cherokee SUV was parked on a slight angle and the brakes gave out at his own home. He was crushed in-between the vehicle and a security gate. The actor had performed the act many times and we're supposed to believe the Jeep's brakes gave out and he could not get out of the way in time? His parents won a lawsuit against the maker of the Jeep Cherokee for an undisclosed settlement. But that does not mean the narrative is true. Very odd (too odd) that the *actor who played Kyle Reese in a Terminator movie was killed by a machine.*

47 The golden statue given out by the Academy of Motion Picture Arts and Sciences actually represents a cock, a dick. Look at it; it's about the right size.

48 Also, what do you think the Golden Globes symbolize? You guessed it: *testicles!* Could these Hollywood institutions be over-compensating?

49 Would you believe who is the oldest person on record, according to the books, that has been shot into space? William (Captain Kirk) Shatner. That's right. The event was seen live in 2023 as the 82-year old actor blasted off and came back to Earth minutes later. This was inside Beso's Elevator-Into-Space that touches the lowest level of space and certainly not in some grand NASA vehicle. He was accompanied by two young rich

dudes who popped champagne upon touchdown. I don't think they knew who Bill Shatner was. The older man took it as a religious experience: "Oooh, the Black! Space was so black!" *I wouldn't buy it for a second.* They were indeed in space and experienced weightlessness for a minute, but this was a public show, folks. For us grounded, poor Earthlings. They have LUXURY SPACESHIPS and have been sending the royalty and their many minion celebrities (children of elites) into space for decades! Don't believe it? Then why did John Lear, of Lear Jets, speak and show evidence of the secret "Aurora" program years before the Shuttle program? If they had specially-privileged people in space decades ago, just exactly what do you think they could do with that futuristic technology today? Keep it for themselves and never share tech or power with all of us little people, not so fortunate. Shatner was acting; he's a good actor.

50 JPL does not stand for the Jet Propulsion Laboratory of NASA. It really stands for 'Jack Parsons Laboratory.' Jack Parsons was a very influential figure in the history of the American space program. He was "a Marxist, stood accused of espionage and held a deep fascination with the Occult." By 1939, Jack and his wife Helen had fully embraced the teachings of Aleister Crowley, considered "the Wickedest Man on Earth." The idea was to achieve a higher state or "true will." In other words: *Anything goes! No laws.* Lines between science and mysticism were crossed as Parsons performed magic rituals, used pentagrams and was a pagan Sun-worshiper.

51 When we say "Parsons" today, we mean the Sheldon-character from TV's 'Big Bang Theory,' Jim Parsons. I'd bet that Jim Parsons is blood-related to Jack Parsons of long ago. Is

that why he got the job? Besides the closeness of their names, we have a genius-character and the many scientific credits of Jack.

52 Jim Parsons had a small but serious role in 'Hidden Figures,' about 3 black women who calculated space flight trajectories in the 1960s. *Don't believe this view of history for a second, folks.* This is Hollywood under England and their job is to lie and only promote a very false Agenda that sways you away from the truth. Strange that Jim Parsons got this part as a bigoted theorist, along with bad reviews. There must be dozens of connections here that are kept hidden from the public. Hidden figures, for sure.

53 *Paul McCartney is really dead!* The very large number of symbols, photos and items on their albums during the band's psychedelic period that suggested Paul's death, were <u>purposely placed there</u>. We will list a myriad of clues that point to the death of one of the original Beatles in 1966. England has always told us in Code what they have done and what they will do. Why would they end their incredible "cash-cow" called the Beatles when they did not have to? Since they [the Royalty] control all Media and your minds, *they can get away with anything~*.

George admitted to it on his deathbed and Ringo did as well in an interview. Now, he's retracted his confession, or is it a Mandela Effect? Ringo was actually recorded when he said: "We thought people would notice, but they didn't, so we just carried on." [But you will no longer find this information on the Internet. Nearly every YouTube criticizes those who believe Paul is dead. *Of course, he's not dead; he's right there alive and kicking!* Oh yeah?].

Clues tell us that the old Paul [2 inches shorter with a rounder face than new Paul] wanted a rhythm and blues band and not a brightly-colored, psychedelic band. He was going to quit, but the Masters of the Beatles made sure that Beatlemania carried on for a few more years. The hidden story is that Paul was angry and "stormed out of a recording studio." His death involved a car-accident, which might not have been an accident. Paul may have been murdered because the Crown had the motive and opportunity to do so. They had a back-up McCartney: the winner of a radio station-sponsored 'Paul Look-Alike Contest.' His name was Billy Shears and he's walking around today as the original McCartney. Not so odd that much of this well-publicized "contest" has been erased.

But they created a William Campbell-character as the replacement Paul that is pure distraction. This is Spy-Stuff and Britain is the master of espionage (lies and deceit). They want you to believe a completely different scenario that Campbell was the new Paul. They and their minions of Media pump out various *red herring* stories that many will believe. But what is the right story and what really happened? Difficult to weed through the BS and know what is real. Let's examine clues that indicate that the original Paul was killed?

54 To set the tone, we have a coincidence that is not a coincidence before what might be a Paul McCartney murder, and that is the Beatles connection with "the Most Wicked Man on Earth": Occultist, Aleister Crowley. Remember how they made the Beatles dress in Wizard costumes? Here's why. Is it a coincidence that the Beatles were posed on the HELP album cover almost exactly as positions laid out in Crowley's book of "Magick"? Certainly not. The Beatles and other rockers (like Bowie, etc, etc.) were always under Dark Influences while we were under the magic spells of singers and musicians.

55 Coincidence that the Beatles put backwards lyrics and music on their later albums [had no choice] and Crowley's proclamation that: "Backwards is the Law." NO.

56 You can toss in Yoda's backwards-speak as well.

57 The British cover for the Beatles' album *Yesterday and Today* showed the Fab Four amid bloody meat and dismembered doll parts, which symbolized the gruesome tragedy. The title meant Yesterday and the new band of Today, without the original Paul.

58 In the song *Taxman,* George Harrison gave his "advice for those who die."

59 Considered maybe the greatest masterwork of music of all time, 'Sgt. Peppers' gave the world a completely different look for the beloved Beatles: Super Technicolor and new sounds inspired by psychedelic mind-stimulants. Released: 5/26/67, this also delineated between the old band and a new one with a new Paul.

60 If one placed a mirror on the 'Lonely Hearts' logo on the Sgt. Peppers cover, you read: '1 ONE 1 X HE DIE 1 ONE 1.'

61 On the back cover of SP, the Beatles are faced forward, but Paul is turned and we only see his back. George Harrison's thumb points to: 'Wednesday morning at 5 o'clock.' When he died. [11/9].

62 At the bottom of the Sgt. Peppers' cover, the Hindu God Shiva, the Destroyer, points at Paul.

63 Side One of SP introduces: *The one and only Billy Shears!!"* just before Ringo's 'With a Little Help from My Friends.' (I thought they sang: "After all these years!!").

64 If there was nothing to this Billy Shears-thing, then why in the movie 'Sgt. Peppers Lonely Hearts Club Band' with the Bee Gees did they have Peter Frampton play Billy Shears?

65 From the song *Day in the Life:* "He blew his mind out in a car. He didn't notice that the lights had changed."

66 A hand is raised over Paul on the cover and this is also a death-symbol.

67 A white toy Aston Martin sits on a doll's knee.

68 (Yes did a song called 'White Car').

69 The yellow flowers form Paul's left-handed bass guitar.

70 One of the 4 strings is missing on Paul's bass.

71 In the song, *She's Leaving Home,* they again repeat the

time of McCartney's death: "Wednesday morning at 5 o'clock as the day begins."

72 On the front cover of 'Magical Mystery Tour,' 3 of them are dressed in white, but the Walrus (posed as if on a cross) is dressed in black. Remember, the Walrus was Paul? In some cultures, a walrus is a symbol of death.

73 On the Magical Mystery Tour, Paul sits at a desk behind a nameplate that read: IWAS (I was).

74 "Aiwass" is another connection to Crowley that students of Crowley will understand.

75 He plays his bass with eyes closed. His blood-stained shoes are nearby.

76 Also in the MMT film, the Beatles are in white tuxedos. They have red flowers on their lapels. Paul McCartney has a black flower.

77 The MMT film ends with GH and JL who watch a strip show with a sleazy stripper and a sleazy nightclub singer. We're distracted by the flash of tits while he sang "Death Cab for Cutie," over and over again. Paul was the *cute one* and again there are car and death references.

78 The title for the band: 'Death Cab for Cutie' (started in 1997) is a direct reference to McCartney's death in 1966.

79 *A Day in the Life* played backwards, you can hear John Lennon who said: "Paul is dead, miss him, miss him."

80 Lennon also said, "I bury Paul" at the end of *Strawberry Fields Forever.*

81 Ringo's drum head in the *I Am the Walrus* video read: 'Love the 3 Beatles.' The boots appear blood-stained.

82 Inside the White Album, a photo shows Paul in a circus-band uniform and on his sleeve there's a O.P.D. patch, which stands for 'Officially Pronounced Dead.'

83 A face of Paul in the booklet where he has on glasses seems a bit different than the other Paul pictures. This is Billy Shears before facial surgery: a "Before Photo."

84 "Octopus' Garden" is a British Navy reference to a graveyard.

85 In the song Revolution #9, played backwards, you can hear: "Turn me on, Dead Man." Also there are sounds of a car crash and an explosion.

86 The Abbey Road cover is filled with a great many clues of McCartney's death: They posed the Beatles perfectly to give the impression this was a *funeral* procession. Gee, wasn't that the same theme as the cover for Sgt. Peppers? Lennon, in white, has been seen as God or the clergy – Ringo in black as a mourner – George in jeans as a gravedigger. Paul was posed without shoes, as many corpses are. Paul has his eyes closed, he is out-of-step with the others and holds a [death-stick] cigarette in the wrong hand.

87 The cover's background contains a VW Beetle (Beatle) with the license plate: LMW27IF, which has been assumed to mean: Linda McCartney Weeps. Paul would be 27 (28) IF he had lived.

Album cover after album cover and song after song contained hints at what Britain had done. (Like their Second World War; the movies about it will never stop). They continuously remind us of their dastardly and covert deeds.

88 The song *Don't Pass Me By* has the line: "You were in a car crash and you lost your hair."

89 Paul McCartney released 'Paul is Live' in 1993. *Really?*

90 It was reported that journalist Jay Marks attended Paul's engagement party in 1967 and was told by a close friend

of the band that *Paul's been replaced.*

91 Representatives of the Beatles have criticized believers that *Paul is really dead.* They've said: "How could the public possibly believe such a thing." Well, maybe it's because everything they've put on their albums and in their songs TOLD US HE WAS DEAD! Was it one big joke on us? Yes. But it's not the joke you think. There is only one of the Beatles that is alive~.

92 Others in the Recording Industry seem to have been told this <u>Big Secret that must be kept</u> along with a vast array of other secrets from the shadows...

93 'The Ballad of Paul' by the Mystery Tour.

94 'Brother Paul' by Billy Shears.

95 'So Long Paul' by Werbley Finster.

96 'Saint Paul' by Terry Knight.

97 'We're All Paul Bearers' by Zacharias and his Tree People.

98 Todd Rundgren's early band, Nazz, recorded a song called 'Hang on Paul' in 1969, 3 years after the "murder" of Paul McCartney. The story is that Paul was a bar-owner he knew. But why do the lyrics sound as if he was giving advice to the New Paul?

*Maybe the GREATEST COINCIDENCE OF ALL TIME might be the fact that "Faux Paul" or Billy Shears, McCartney's taller replacement, just so happened to have *more natural musical ability than the original Paul! Truly Unbelievable Serendipity!*

~We have all been TRICKED by their Magical Tour.

99 Why is Hollywood called "Hollywood"? Magic, the fine art of Deception. "Pay no attention to the man behind the curtain." Witches use wands made from the holly plant. The

holy Holly Plant is dioecious: the bushes are either male or female, which is very rare in the Plant Kingdom. Hemp or pot is one other rare plant that displays the sexes, physically. We can visually tell a male from a female, but in about all other cases, male and female plants look the same. Now consider the pushed bisexuality within the realm of the Movie Industry. Or the pushed Witchcraft? Coincidence?

100 Closely examine the cover of *Supertramp's Breakfast in America* album that is reversed. This is one of the best examples of Predictive Programming. Not an accident or a bizarre coincidence. Notice directly above the Twin Towers of what is obviously New York City: We can clearly view '**911**.' The album was released on March 16, 1979. If we pull back, we discover that we're actually looking out of an airplane window. On the back of the album, there's a drawing of a jet heading for NY. There are photos of the band having breakfast and looking at newspapers. That's exactly what all of us did that Tuesday morning in 2001, watched the news reports. Coincidences?

101 The original cover for rap group *The Coup's* album called 'Party Music' was created in June of 2001. It showed Boots Riley and Pam the Funkstress *destroying the Twin Towers of the World Trade Center,* apparently using a detonator! The release date of the CD was delayed 2 months from early September, 2001, to November.

102 The third live album by *Dream Theater* was actually released on SEPTEMBER 11, 2001! The cover shows an Apple wrapped in barbed wire with the NYC skyline engulfed in flames. The band was forced to change the cover and publicly say it was only a *"coincidence."*

103 An American band called *Squad Five-0* released their third album: 'Bombs Over Broadway' in 2000. World War 2 bombers were seen flying low over NYC with the Twin Towers in view. The album's lyrics also indicated the attacks: "Up in flames." "Ground zero" and "We never saw it coming."

104 The X-Files spinoff series *The Lone Gunmen* had, in their pilot episode, a Boeing 727 passenger plane that flew toward the Twin Towers with the intention of *crashing into a tower!* Only in the last moment, TLG were able to hack the hacker and avoid the disaster. The pilot episode was aired in Australia just 13 days before the events of 9/11.

105 Where was President Bush when the planes attacked that Tuesday morning in New York City? (Why does everything start on Tuesday, like school?). He was in a Florida schoolroom with a teacher and her students. He was informed that a plane struck one of the Twin Towers and he carried on with the students as if nothing had happened. The teacher made the children sound out words written on a blackboard. The words were "steel" and "plane" and "must." Was any of this coincidence? At the exact moment of the attack, these words were written? Absolutely not coincidences.

106 Star Trek and 2001: A Space Odyssey's connection to the events of 9/11. What? Well, 2001 is an obvious connection that we believe is not connected. Why 2001? Why not 1999, or 2000 or 2002? No, it had to be 2001. From the '60s, it was a stamp imprinted on our psyches...that special year of 2001. I would bet the farm that those [group] who blank-checked Kubrick's films and maybe the charade that was the Moon Landing, also caused the world-shaking event in NY that morning. Star Trek. What does NCC-1701 mean? The trekkers know what I'm talking about: the letters/numbers on the U.S.S. Enterprise space vessel with Captain Kirk in command. It was always there and little understood by millions of outsiders not in the secret club, not on the other side of Hollywood's Curtain. Numerology tells us simply that NCC is 5+3+3=11. Add 1+7+0+1=9. Reverse the code and you have **9/11.** I would bet just about anything that the greatest TV sci-fi series and the greatest sci-fi movie were meant to conceal what *they* planned, the destruction of the NY Twin Towers.

107 In the Bible, Boaz and Jachin were 2 side-by-side pillars on the porch of Solomon's Temple. They are referenced repeatedly in Masonic material. NY Twin Towers symbolized those towers?

108 Was it a strange coincidence that on that infamous day of December 7, 1941, all of the American naval ships were parked at Pearl Harbor, on the island of Oahu? President Franklin Roosevelt, the Commander-in-Chief of U.S. military forces, ordered (was ordered) to have all naval ships at Pearl Harbor for "inspection." This was precisely when the Japanese Air Force struck! Normally, you'd never send your forces into one spot. Of course, eastern spies could have discovered this

fact and knew this was prime time to strike. But, the narrative we've been told is not what clearly happened. **Britain caused the attack to occur** as they have fooled the world again and again. They are the money-printers and Controllers of every aspect of our lives and for generations before our time. It was too convenient that the PH attack was exactly what the United Kingdom wanted: to drag our country into the war they had created. With the Royalty's firm control of its celebrities and movies and Media promotions, it was easily achieved. America had no choice. Any resistance or peace movements were destroyed. We were going to war, whether we wanted to or not. This was just what happened in the First World War, we were forced into Europe's War! Why not do it all over again? And it happened, was made to happen.

109 By this logic, Hitler was a creation of England. A controlled, mad monster that everyone was made to fear. And he was. Hitler played the perfect part on the "stage" of war, aka "the theatre of war." English Royalty needed an enemy to frighten the world, so they created one.

110 It also was too convenient that when the Nazis attacked England with their Blitzkrieg in 1940, they did not think to destroy where the leaders of Britain were located? German aircraft did not bomb Parliament, London Bridge, Big Ben, Whitehall or Balmoral Castle? No. If the Big War was a real war, that would be where Nazis would have struck. Instead, they bombed the people, the London underground. *This horrible act greatly favored the Royal Elites and did not hurt them in the least. There were now less people that did not have to be on the "dole" after the war.*

111 Adolph Hitler had dark eyes and a unique mustache,

a vertical 'stash that went up and down. The only other person at the time that had a mustache like Hitler's was Charlie Chaplin, who played a Hitler-character in 'The Great Dictator.' Very strangely now, everything's been changed and Hitler has blue, sympathetic eyes? His mustache (and Chaplin's) now resemble Stalin's and is considerably bushier. Does the change mean that Hitler was not unique anymore, not a freak monster, but an Everyman? That's true only in a dark, warped world.

112 Jerry Seinfeld and Superman. Guess why Jerry was into Superman~. Considered (pushed to be) one of the greatest TV shows ever, Seinfeld mentioned Superman a number of times and had a picture of him on his fridge and a statue on a shelf. The creators of the show even produced a "Bizarro" episode [from Superman] with reverse/parallel versions of themselves. The new group were nice and the original 4 were not. Why bring in the universe of the Bizarro Superman where right is wrong, wrong is right, 'hello' is 'good-bye' and the reverse is true, etc.? No one knew in the '90s how topsy-turvy, backwards and upside-down the next decades would become. *But the creators of the show knew!* They knew because THEY, who rule and determine the world, are the ones who manipulate our world from the shadows. A covert Agency creates everything big on the World Stage as well as a multitude of small things through their Media minions. It is not bizarre that this happened, it is very *normal* in a twisted world.

113 It is not a coincidence that federal "epidemic director" Dr. Anthony Fauci has been found to be wrong or "falsey." Was it set up to be this way from the beginning? Yes.

114 Also, not a coincidence that Tony Fauci resembles a Nazi. You haven't noticed? If you wanted to cast a Nazi in a

movie, you'd cast someone like the "good" doctor: a small, rat-faced person with round, wire-rimmed glasses.

115 The Coronavirus. Why did they wait until the year 2020 to unleash the virus upon us? A virus that was not a Death Sentence as first reported, but a flu you got over in a few days. Why not another year? *Nothing Big Just Happens!* There's Code in just about everything they [the Monarchy] have established and do. The "2020" reference is *seeing clearly;* we see clearly when we have 2020 eyesight. But they made sure that no one saw clearly back at the beginning of 2020 and drastically threw us off-balance. No outsider understood what was really happening around them: the helicopters, the masks, the restrictions, the mandates and basically, the FEAR that was implanted inside everyone.

116 Why the change of name from the 'Coronavirus' to 'Covid'? Might it have to do with British diversionary tactics? Maybe the source for the virus was not China or some eastern country? Maybe it was from the old Corona Road in London?

117 Courtrooms. Why do *all* courtrooms, no matter the country, have a wooden gate that the accused must pass through before they sit on the stand? It means: you are *cattle* behind a metaphoric fence, and if you step through, you must abide by the court's decisions. In other words, if you step through...you're *hamburger*

118 Nemesis in the courtroom. There is a statue of Justice in about every courtroom. Sometimes the Lady holds a sword, sometimes she holds balance scales or both. Wait, she's Justice? Then why is she *blindfolded?* How do you render fair justice when you cannot see all the facts? She stands there in every

courtroom and even TV courtrooms...*blindfolded?* That's your symbol? That's what they've done to Justice (Nemesis)? Yes. Truth is it accurately represents the *injustice* that has always been throughout world legal systems.

119 So, Pluto isn't a planet anymore? Bullshit. This has been an insidious plot by the British International Astronomical Union. The shocker these days is just about everybody accepts this crap. Insane and irrational views and actions are not questioned anymore. People, more the youth, simply accept what's being forcefed to them over and over again. They do not realize that the authorities, through Media, LIE to us! They lie so much it's like they are not lying at all. *It's everywhere.* Garbage is promoted and taken as truth and the real Truth is something so far removed from what "They say."

Examine the real photo here, one of numerous photographs which are very difficult to find on the Internet in these times:

This is Pluto after the whitewash or masking that NASA does to prevent us from seeing what is really there is removed. Note the regular patterns. Nothing in nature is in these squared and rectangular patterns such as what's seen over farmlands. Pluto is not super-cold. Pluto has two relatively large moons that have a unique relationship. Could it be that the International

Astronomical Union knows all about the ALIEN ACTIVITY in and around planet Pluto? And that's why they have declared it not a planet? "Don't even look at it; there's nothing there. "

120 There is a satellite of Saturn named Pandora. It was discovered in 1980 by the Voyager I probe. In 1985, it was officially named "Pandora." Pandora was also the home world of the blue monkey creatures in the film 'Avatar.' I wonder if there is life in the jungles of Pandora? I'm not saying the natives are blue. Maybe they're green?

121 *The Shining,* Stanley Kubrick's confession in a film. James Cameron has publicly stated that Stanley Kubrick faked the Moon landing with "front-screen projection," the same as what was used in the primate scene of '2001.' Many investigators of *The Shining* have concluded that where Kubrick deviated from Stephen King's book was where he placed hints of what he had done for King and Country. Jack Nicholson's character is introduced to the Overlook Hotel by a character played by Barry Nelson in a JFK wig. He is supposed to look like President Kennedy who was instrumental in the U.S. space program. Nelson also played the first James Bond, before Sean Connery (on American live TV). His casting might have something to do with all of the spy-stuff going on in Kubrick's mind. Items in the office also hint of the space program (flag, eagle). Son Danny wore an APOLLO 11 sweater the whole time, in plain sight. The long tapestries on the wall near the beginning had rocket designs on them. The hexagon shapes in the carpet were meant to mimic the designs of launch pads. The television was on but no wire was attached to it, which represented the surreal reality we viewed. Stanley changed the frightening room # in the film to Room 237.

According to James Cameron, that was the # of the stage where Kubrick faked the Moon landing. It is also the distance to the Moon: 237,000 miles. Stephen King was supposedly outraged at the changes in the film version. For example, the family's original car was a red VW Beetle in the book. But when Dick Halloran, the caretaker, drove over a snowy road, he saw a semi-truck that had crushed a red VW bug. This was the director's way of saying to the author, "We're doing it my way and your way has been trashed." The filmmaker was given lenses only NASA used for this film and later films. Kubrick's changes revealed his emotional turmoil with his "Deal with the Devil."

122 'Dr. Strangelove or: How I Learned to Stop Worrying and Love the Bomb' (1964). Kubrick was a little too accurate with his interpretation of inside a cockpit of a B-29 bomber that he shouldn't have known. The story is his research team did their jobs too well and they were about to be investigated by the FBI. Reason tells us: Stanley Kubrick was never in trouble with the feds, rather he was an obedient servant for the Monarchy and given the *Keys to the Kingdom* (blank checks).

123 Shouldn't the "War Room" be called the "Peace Room"?

124 Scientology. Is it so strange that L. Ron Hubbard wrote sci-fi and then created basically a tax-exempt Religion? I mean a *kooky* religion, to say the least, when you find out the basic principle behind it. His flock of followers, many celebrities like Tom Cruise and John Travolta, pay big bucks to use bio-feedback machines, then to have invisible eels or "thetans" removed from their bodies. The deeper you travel into the depths of Scientology, you discover the origin of people on

Earth (right?). *Spoiler:* Lord Xenu was the dictator of a Galactic Confederacy of 76 planets. He was imprisoned 75 million years ago after he brought billions of people to Earth. Xenu placed the people inside volcanoes and then killed them with hydrogen bombs. *[Boy, I certainly can't write fiction like that]*. Scientologists are shocked when they reach these deep levels, that this is what they have to believe is the truth? Hubbard has to be the greatest conman since Aleister Crowley.

125 Today's leader of Scientology and hero to Tom Cruise is a man named David Miscavige. Sounds a lot like "miscarriage," doesn't it? Is it a "miscarriage of justice"? The real mystery is what happened to his wife, Michelle "Shelly" Miscavige? She has not made a public appearance since August 2007 and this has become the source of much speculation.

126 What's the connection between famous filmmakers George Lucas, Francis Ford Coppola and Stephen Spielberg? The conception was they met in film school, but now we discover that Spielberg never went to film school? How'd they meet? Each have become elite filmmakers where about everything they touched have turned to gold. Many strange parallels between the three. But I'm talking about the beards. *So ahead of their times?* Wouldn't you have one moment in your life where you'd change? Artists are supposed to change. <u>Why not shave</u>? [My message to the world]. The conclusion must be that these famous guys, like almost everyone today, **must have beards**! It is a requirement of Slavery, like tattoos: badges they must wear (and baldness) to please their Slave Masters on high levels above.

127 We are all slaves, but we don't have to look like slaves. Wait. Apparently...you *do* have to look like slaves. *Look*

at you! See with your eyes what the young people of today look like: bald, bearded, covered in ugly tattoos and only know to wear black? You used to have the "gangsta-look," back in the '90s, but now it's the Slave-Look. You have not taken great leaps forward into the Future, people, you have been driven backwards and are now locked into Medieval Dungeons. Where are the dragons? Is Jon Snow your King? What's next? A movement that places you further back into caves?

128 Coincidence that black people now star in movies, star in TV shows, commercials, get jobs over white people? And this has all been decreed by the *whitest people on Earth:* British Royals.

129 Strange that, long ago, it was primarily men who received medical scholarships to Medical Schools, but now *far more women are given the scholarships.* In future, you won't see men doctors anymore. (There are always a few exceptions).

130 Isn't it funny, odd, strange, that women are now seen in All-Media, in all films and commercials as STRONG, FULL OF KNOWLEDGE and very POWERFUL Warriors, even killers. Certainly not the gentler of the sexes. Not even young girls are sweet anymore. Not in movies or anywhere around us. (And not in our minds). This is no coincidence or natural climate where men now take passive roles, inferior to women. No, this is *forced* by those in High Towers who control our Minds through all forms of Media. The reason "women" celebrities and *lady* action-stars are so violent and tough is because they are MEN "under the skin." The reason "men" celebrities (also down to D-List stars) are so very passive and submissive is because they are really WOMEN "under the skin."

131 The #1 "female" tennis player for the last few years has been Iga Swiatek from Poland. She dominates the lady's tour with a powerful game. She has the chest of a man. But pay attention to the symbol printed on her chest and her ball cap: It is the logo for the *On Cloud* shoe company that sponsors her.

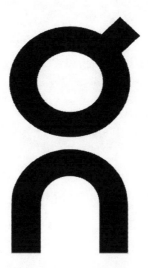

On Cloud company says they want to give the impression of "running on clouds." They feature "...the letters 'O' and 'N' stacked on top of one another in black and white print." What? Does this logo in any way convey the idea of cloud running? That's an "O"? No, it isn't; it's a Male Symbol that no one seems to see. Iga is the first "female" sponsored by the shoe company. Why the notch on the "O" that makes the symbol male? Is Iga a man, like the Williams Sisters have been proven to be through trans-vestigations? I've done commercial art logos and that image reminds me of one drop of semen that popped up out of a cockhead. I have a feeling Joe Camel would agree.

132 On this one, examine the shoulders and neck of two star athletes: 1) Caitlin Clark, the college phenom basketball player that now plays in the WNBA...and Lamar Jackson,

quarterback for the Baltimore Ravens. Caitlin has been pushed and pushed by sports shows, not because of her super play on the basketball court – it is because of the secret club-factory that she emerged from. Notice her long (male) neck and extremely masculine shoulders. No wonder she's great at the 3-point shot. Now, take a good look at Lamar Jackson without shoulder pads on. The severe A-frame house-angle to his small shoulders is reminiscent of females. Where's his neck? [Those giraffe-like supermodels weren't women. That's (Queen) 'Victoria's Secret.' And those no-neck muscle-men weren't men].

133 Ever wonder why celebrities always marry or partner with other celebrities? Just a coincidence that two famous people find true love? In the real world, that would never be the case. Your spouse might often be on a movie-shoot in another country a lot of the time. Why have your children always in the hands of a nanny? You'd never want a famous boyfriend or wife if you didn't have to be with them, forced to be with them. You'd want a *not-famous* person to partner with. One that loves you and worships the ground you walk on and takes good care of your children. Why can't we find one? Maybe there's one or two? But there should not be only a few exceptions. That should be the rule or the norm and on rare/rare occasions would a celebrity ever be mated with another celebrity. Right? No, it's the other way around in Lalaland. The obvious reason is Club Members know the Big Secret and also agents and handlers direct their lives.

134 Not so strange or wrong that decades ago (when afternoon talk shows were interesting) on 'Cavett,' Gloria Swanson clearly stated: "In Germany, **in the 1920s**, they were

making the most beautiful boys out of girls and making the most beautiful girls out of boys." She would know; she was one of the "It" girls when she was young. "I'm ready for my close-up, Mr. DeMille."

135 Why do so many tennis professionals and other celebrities wear CROSSES? Certainly not because they are religious. Maybe it's a fashion statement? Or maybe it's another requirement for elite minions from those who run the world? There's too many crosses worn by insincere people who are hypocrites. Why not wear them under your clothes and keep your (false) imagery and beliefs to yourself? Why do they show them off like billboards and make others feel inferior? Here's the truth. It is one more thing that needs to be decoded. *Crosses mean cross-gender.* Not in all cases, but in a lot of cases of the rich/famous, we are being deceived by Masters of Deception. For more than 100 years, England has instituted certain requirements for its minion slaves that they utterly control, 100%. They dole out fame and fortune to the slaves that obey them the most. For example, why give the Academy Award to a great actor who is really a man, when a woman secretly playing a man would be a far greater acting achievement? It's one reason the world is upside-down and trannies are everywhere. Elites are not the gender that they appear. (Serena Williams?). But they are made to always push or mention their children, from motherhood to fatherhood. Too much. More over-compensation?

136 Why does almost every single pro tennis player wear CHAINS? I was an amateur player on a college scholarship in tennis and have played most of my life. I would never play with chains or jewelry or even a penny in my pocket. Why? It makes

no sense for pros who play for millions of dollars. But they *all* wear chains, with only a very few players who must be exempt from the required chains. Now, decode: The meaning is SLAVERY, the chains of slavery. Pros, as children, are slaves to the tennis Industry [factory] and are forced/trained into their profession by their Masters or parents who *push* them (not fair to ordinary people). Elite children receive the best training in every field. Almost all are forced by the age of 6 to perform at their highest level. This is really child abuse and too much pressure for a very young person to deal with. Wouldn't one up and coming tennis pro not wear chains? See if you can find one? You (almost) won't be able to.

137 There was a YouTube video that revealed an astonishing coincidence: Kim Clijsters was a top tennis pro at the time and she held in her lap a 5-year old child on the grounds of the U.S. Open. The very young child was Sofia Kenin who won (given) a major pro tennis tournament much later in 2020, the Australian Open. She said, in a tiny voice: "I want to win the U.S. Open like Andy Roddick." The video was posted to show this oddity, but, Insiders know better. It was not a coincidence at all. Kim Clijsters (future "mom") was intended to show elite-child Sofia everything, the courts, locker room, the Press room, the tennis stars and basically convey the idea: *All of this can be yours; just do what they tell you to do.*

138 German-born John McEnroe just happened to be a ball-boy at the 1974 U.S. Open when he was 15...then went on to be one of the greatest tennis players of his era. You think that was a coincidence? No way. They were "grooming" him like they have groomed many other proteges.

139 The (terrible/terrible) game of 'Pickleball' has been

forced and pushed upon us. How could this have happened?! It's an awful tragedy that park tennis courts are being replaced by fucking Pickleball courts in major cities over the whole planet! *Pickleball!?* It's not a coincidence that the game was named after something green that stinks!

140 **I invented a lineless, singles, tennis court** 20 years ago called "Roval" that had nothing straight in its design. Look it up. A whole page with picture was published in Tennis Week Magazine in 2005 with Rafa Nadal on the cover. Nick Bollettieri wished me good luck with it. He hoped, like I did, that it might be accepted on the grounds of the U.S. Open (for fun, to attract crowds). But the British International Tennis Federation wrote to me and said: "We cannot support a game that purports to replace tennis." *It wasn't going to replace tennis, it was going to stand alongside it!* I find it curious to the extreme that the bastards at the ITF have chosen to get behind fucking Pickleball! It is actually, literally, replacing tennis in parks and country clubs. *Madness!* It's everywhere, now. A TV commercial just ran and told the audience: "Hey, it's Pickleball season!" There's even now 'Pickleball TV." NO, NO, NO, NOOO!!

ROVAL singles court with **NO LINES!**

Serves must hit the center Soval to be good, BUT, as soon as that happens & the point begins, the Soval is an OUT area, painted same as outside of court. In this way, singles is played without lines. No foot-faults, can step into a longer court.

141 Is it a coincidence or just a darn shame that England still insists on not displaying the Russian flag along with the name of Russian sports figures in graphics? For example, Mirra Andreeva and Aryna Sabalenka just played in the women's French Open semi-final and neither could have their country's flag next to their names. The players are not at fault and have nothing to do with politics. Why are they penalized? England rules tennis and also rules the world: *They completely control Russia and the United States!* More than ironic since the Monarchy's social-engineers have produced all wars and are behind all military strikes.

142 Stefanos Tsitsipas is a professional tennis player from Greece (Greek fisherman) who appears like you might think Jesus Christ would look today with semi-long hair. His father is named "Apostolos." He's his son's #1 Apostle and coach. And Stefanos' mother, a former tennis champion, is also there during his matches. So we have the whole "holy" family.

143 Is it a coincidence that Rafa Nadal, one of the greatest tennis players, comes from Soccer Royalty? His uncle, Miguel Angel Nadal, was a very talented football player and played for FC Barcelona and Mallorca. Just a coincidence, no?

144 Jannik SINNER is a top, young tennis player who has just received the Number 1 ranking in the world. He's an Italian and has been highly promoted by the Associated Press in Rome. Odd that the "Holy City" supports Mr. Sinner?

145 Is it a coincidence that the greatest tennis player of all time, with 24 major tournament wins, Novak Djokovic...and the greatest basketball player of the last few years, Nikola Jokic, both have the same nickname? "Joker."

146 It's a little too odd that in Star Trek there are aliens called the Cardassians...and you have the reality-television show 'The Kardashians.' Think they're not connected? Examine the patriarch of this brood, he was one of O.J. Simpson's lawyers. Look at his distinctive hair. Now look at the hair they placed on Cardassian aliens. Every Cardassian has the same hair and it's *Robert's hair!* Odd that Bruce Jenner is a tranny? He may be a female-to-male-to-female? "Yeah, baby."

147 A very strong resemblance has been recognized between Pope Benedict XVI and Emperor Palpatine in Star Wars sequels, otherwise known as Darth Sidious. Is this a coincidence or is there something going on with the similarity? Is the Pope the Phantom Menace?

148 Did Prince predict his own death? In his song, 'Let's Go Crazy,' the lyrics talk of *Death* and the "After World." But the song begins as if we're in church: "Dearly beloved. We are gathered here today to get through this thing called life." Some of the lyrics: "And if the Elevator tries to bring you down." "Are we going to let the Elevator bring us down?" "We're all gonna die." "Grim Reaper." As mentioned later, Prince was found dead in his own *elevator* at his Paisley Park estate.

149 32 and 33. Take a good look at sports figures who wore the numbers 32 and 33. The best examples are listed. This connects to freemasonry as initiates work up the degrees and the ritual ends at the 33rd level. Presidents have been reported to be either 32 or 33 degree freemasons. Isn't it odd that many of the best players on professional teams just happen to wear 32 or 33? These are often the best player on the team by far and sure Hall of Famers:

32: Shaquille O'Neal, Magic Johnson, Jim Brown, Julius Erving, O.J. Simpson, Sandy Koufax, Karl Malone, Marcus Allen, Franco Harrris, Dave Winfield, Bill Walton, Kevin McHale, Jack Tatum, Ricky Watters, Jason Kidd, Claude Lemieux, Steve Carlton, Jamal Anderson and Jack Pardee.

33: Kareem Abdul-Jabbar, Larry Bird, Shaquille O'Neal, Scottie Pippen, Frank Robinson, Patrick Ewing, Tony Dorsett, Roger Craig, Alonzo Mourning, Eddie Murray, Earl Monroe, Grant Hill, Mike Piazza, Vida Blue and Jose Canseco.

150 'The Number 23' was a 2007 film that starred Jim Carrey. A few well-known sports figures have worn this special number: Michael Jordan, LeBron James, Anthony Davis, Ron Artest, Draymond Green, Don Mattingly and Jimmy Butler.

151 One more connection of a thing that we would normally think is not connected: The National Football League's new extra-point that was instituted back in 2015. This was to make the game more interesting with a longer extra-point that is more likely to be missed. It was on the 15-yard line. Where to move it to make the kick longer? [I actually predicted this and am quite proud of the achievement]. Fans might say: the 20-yard line or the 25-yard line. Nope. It was moved to and will permanently stay on the *23-yard line.* Why?

Because with a 23-yard kick, one has to add 10 more yards to the goal post. The new 23-yard extra point is actually 33 yards and is because of their honoring the number: "33." {Jesus' age when *they* murdered him}.

152 Inverted names of famous people. We don't notice how many famous people have first names as last names. We think there is no connection when there definitely is. This goes with the inverted, backwards nature of things that has been forced upon us. Names like Elton John, LeBron James, Michael Jordan, Dean Martin, Jerry Lewis, Pete Rose, Jimmy Stewart, Kirk Douglas, Jack Benny, Ray Charles, Jane Seymour, Hugh Grant, Babe Ruth, Caitlin Clark, Chris Paul, Spike Lee, Danica Patrick, Kyrie Irving, Larry David, Emmanuel Lewis, George Will, Carly Simon, Steve Allen, Susan Oliver, Tommy Kirk... It's endless. A disproportionate amount of celebrities have first names as last names. Coincidences? Not at all.

153 Another oddity is that movie titles that mention gender such as Superman, Batman, Batgirl, The Prince and the Showgirl, Boystown, And God Created Women, Girls Night Out, Our Man Flint, His Girl Friday, Spice Girls, Midnight Cowboy, Where the Boys Are, Men of Honor, That Girl, New Girl, Men in Space, etc. are filled with actors that have not passed trans-investigations. One example is Gal Gadot who plays Wonder Woman. The clue is "her" first name. Not a gal. Remember Boy George? Not a boy.

154 In Hollywood movies, the characters repeatedly refer to their own gender. Too many times, over and over again: "I'm not that kind of woman." "I'm your man." "I'm the right man for the job." "What kind of a girl do you take me for?" "A woman like me should be insulted." "What's a guy supposed to

do?" - on and on... No one talks like that in real life. But in the world of Movies, they keep emphasizing their genders as if we don't know? *And we don't know,* for the most part.

155 Isn't it a weird oddity that Anne Rice, many times, got the title wrong of her own book at the Oscars when her book was made into a movie that starred Tom Cruise and Brad Pitt? She wasn't drunk. This was a Mandela Effect; she got it right. But the Universe has now changed the title of the book and the movie to: 'Interview With The Vampire.' A lot of people clearly remember the book and movie were originally called 'Interview With A Vampire,' with a bright red '<u>A</u>' on book covers and film posters. I saw it in the theater and knew it well.

156 Was it also a weird oddity that Gwen Stefani, Julia Roberts, George Clooney and James Cordon were just riding around listening to Queen's 'We are the Champions' and were SURPRISED that the end of the song did not have "OF THE WORLD!"? No, no, they were acting. They knew very well what their Masters had done to the planet long before this moment. Don't act surprised. The last 3 words to the song, that everyone remembers, is no longer there, and *never* been there? Does the absence of those words mean the Old World is not here anymore?

157 Wasn't it really bizarre that actor Hugh Grant was caught receiving oral sex from a "sex worker," Divine Brown, in his car on Hollywood's Sunset Boulevard in 1995? His British movie 'Sense and Sensibility' had been released and the young *man* was at the height of his popularity. The actor could have walked into any bar and *left with ten women!* He could have easily paid for a few Call Girls. Why stoop so low, get caught and tarnish his brand in Hollywood? Why take the

chance? Because he's kinky? Once you know how "sacrifices" work behind the Curtain of fame and fortune, then you might understand? He had no choice. This was his sacrifice.

158 The Pee-wee Herman scandal. "Have you heard any good jokes lately?" The exact same can be said for Paul Reubens, aka Pee-wee Herman. There was already a dick-joke in the comedian's name. As the story goes, Mr. Reubens was caught masturbating in a porn theater in 1991 and arrested for "indecent exposure." Really? Since when do police officers make spot-checks inside porn theaters? Everyone believed it. And this was not a set-up, a *sacrifice* that the actor had to perform? If Pee-wee Herman walked into any bar, he could have left with *a babe on either arm!* Who wouldn't want to boink Pee-wee and then tell their friends all about it later? One more event that did not simply happen, but was made to happen. You'll have a hit TV show, star in movies and have the adoration of everyone, Pee-wee. But one day, you will have to pay for all of your good fortune.

159 You can also make a strong case for the downfall of Bill Cosby. Cosby and his kids. He had hit comedy albums, starred in 'I Spy' and did the 'Fat Albert' animated series. Later, *The Cosby Show* was the top sit-com on television. He had a popular novel on the NY Best-Seller's List, 'Fatherhood.' Bill had a movie career. Everyone loved Bill Cosby...that was until a few dozen women (accusers) came forward in 2015 and wanted the famous man prosecuted for drugging them and raping them. Now, there are a number of fishy things here: 1) Did Bill Cosby have to use Rohypnol ("date-rape drug") to have affairs and cheat on Camille? *He's freaking Bill Cosby!* I don't believe he needed to do what he was accused of to get laid. 2) Take a good

look at his accusers. Yes, they are considerably older, but they are not very attractive. Wouldn't pretty young ladies age into decent-looking older women? Not in this case. They appear quite butch. Some of the accusers have been trans-vestigated and did not pass the gender-test. So what's really going on here, people? Could the entire downfall of Cosby and the trial be just one more [fake news, tranny] *sacrifice* required by the Masters of the World?

160 Rap Music. Again, what's in a name? Ever wonder why Rap Music is called "Rap"? In the '60s and '70s, "rap" meant to stay up late and talk or just have a discussion. But today, and for the last 30 years, the term means a certain kind of music: *The last phase of music that will ever be!* Rap is the Undying Monster that will never go away. Pushed. It's everywhere and it's been forced to be everywhere for decades. Cool, huh? Not cool. Anyone can be a rap-star, you don't even have to be able to sing. Are bands that are super, instrumentally, like on guitars or keyboards, promoted and praised anymore? No. You don't even have to know how to play musical instruments anymore. Where is the next movement in music? Nowhere. *[Don't give me rave Bass-Music, it sucks].* Everything has always cycled and returned again in a different form. For example, '80s music was a revisit of bright/colorful music of the '60s. Today? Great music is dead and will never ever return to us again. There is no color; it's all black. *Rap* actually (to Insiders) means 'wrap.' As in a wrap-party: The End. "Wrap it up. It's over."

161 Why has hashish disappeared from legal pot stores over the last few years? Hash was readily available and sold in a wide range of varieties: blonde hash, dark hash, domestic

hash, Lebanese hash, powdery hash or 'thick as a brick' hash. Today, *gone!* You see, hash is concentrated hemp: you cannot extract the active ingredient in marijuana (THC) from it. But from a normal/potent bud (flower) of pot, you can extract the precious THC that gets you high and also is an essential element in pot's *industrial uses*. The finest paper, fabrics, linen, paints, varnishes, soaps, salves, shampoos, skin lotions and other very expensive products found behind locked cases in some stores. What if the government (always directed to – under orders) extracted the special (sauce) THC from all the buds in federal stores and used them for these high-end products? Then sprayed these beautiful-looking plant buds with a fragrance that simulated a potent bud of weed? What if they, the feds, fooled us totally years ago when they completely took over the Marijuana Industry, as it was planned from the beginning? Decent/caring growers, down through the decades, fought the good fight for the legalization of pot. We did not vote for government regulations! THE LIE is pot dispensaries might sell pot that harms the public. Growers would never do that: put paraquat or harmful agents on the pot that they sold? It would not be good for business. There were no outbreaks of anything bad in those first and very wonderful years of legal pot. But the government came in and the only stores that were allowed to operate and deal with the public were federal stores. The fastest growing business was shutdown; *store after store after store had to close down.* In the first days, PEOPLE were in charge and dispensaries had No Tax. Pot came in bags or plastic containers. Cheap prices. A large variety. They sold different types of hash. (Hash, which is easy to make). Stores were fun places to visit and the sellers almost appeared as hippies. Games, and pot-prizes you could win! Today, pot stores are not safe places to buy weed because the pot might be harmful to smoke. The sellers are all in black and covered in tattoos. Dispensaries are not fun/colorful places anymore. Prices are high. Limited selections. Buds in glass jars with a protective lid that is difficult to open. They're placed in an unnecessary box. All the information about it, like its potency, is written on the label. Don't believe a word of it. People would not sell harmful marijuana. *But the government would!* And every safety measure they have insisted upon should tell the intelligent person: *They are insisting too much. This is not good weed.* I seriously believe (through experience) the pot you buy now does not work, is no longer a medicine and might even be harmful to our system. Maybe people only *think* they are getting high on it? It might be like how a placebo works. A sorry state of affairs, if it is true? But look around you in the world...haven't *They* ruined everything?

162 By the same token, many years ago, farms/farmlands were completely taken over by the feds, and they were also under orders to do so. Sixty years ago, when the youth were naive, full of dreams and were positive...a hippie culture existed that wanted to live off the land. Own a farm and provide food to those who need food at fair prices. Dreams and freedoms of Americans and a lot of other people have been lined-up in a firing squad and SHOT DEAD! No store is permitted to sell food grown by ordinary people. Even large farms must be federally owned. Everything must be regulated by federal inspectors. No matter how large and beautiful your homegrown tomatoes were, you could never sell them to the small, mom and pop store on the corner (like you could long ago). Now, this is all well and good if you really produced clean and safe food-products. But NEWSFLASH: Food has not been safe, really

safe for consumption, in decades. The feds must spray numerous types of pesticides on all of what the federal farms produced. The farmers must get into thick, protective suits so they won't be adversely affected by the spray intended to kill bugs, etc. They're in helmets with suits that appear as radiation suits, which indicate the dangers of such pesticides. *And we eat the food?!* There are probably mechanical means that apply the spray today, but the fact remains: All of it must get dosed and there are no exceptions. Is the water safe to drink? Is the air safe to breathe? Can we really trust federal authorities who might only be carrying out orders from not the best of sources?

163 Why no free restaurants? Free food! Not one person in a civilized society should be homeless or go hungry. Wouldn't you think one billionaire would create a chain of restaurants that served quality food and it was FREE to the public? For tax purposes, to be taken off their high taxes? Doesn't that make sense? Or a group of millionaires? Or some organization that claims to do good in the world and aid those less fortunate? (There are a few churches that do charity work and pass out free food to the poor, but who says it is good food?). Not one rich person will do this? The reason they cannot is: The Mafia or whatever Secret Society runs this department in the world. They own the Restaurant Industry, probably worldwide, and "protect" them. With establishments that offered free/quality food, there would be lines and lines of people. The Restaurant bosses will not allow such free eateries. And lose business? No way. And if some upstart wanted to defy them and open a Free Restaurant...then, in no time, rats would be found in those places and control of the (bad) Press would soon crush them! *The anagram for "restaurant" is "eat, rats run."*

164 Was it a coincidence that less than a month after the horrendous damage caused by Hurricane Katrina in 2005...another weather-event called Hurricane Rita hit the same area and was even more destructive?! [Nikola Tesla developed machines that controlled the weather. He meant them to be used positively, constructively, not like how the feds have used them (HAARP)]. There were reports at the time that suggested these hurricanes were not natural because of their high intensity and their odd movements. Both events moved in strange patterns that hurricanes normally do not do – as if they were being directed, tested, controlled by a remote source? If there was nothing to "Weather Wars," then why did the United Nations outlaw "weather modification" on 5/18/77? The agreement was signed in Geneva, Switzerland.

165 Funny that the United Kingdom does not allow its subjects to have guns. Interesting. (In their American colony or "corporation," it's *Anything Goes!)*. For the longest time, not even the police carried guns in the UK. I assume if the English royalty allowed guns among the citizens, there might not be much of the Monarchy left.

*Is it a coincidence that the character Raymond Burr played in the original *Godzilla* movie was named 'Steve Martin,' the same as the popular comedian who burst on the scene 20 years later? YES. I think that this is a real coincidence. *There has only been a few real coincidences, people.*

Simpsons' Predictions?

"Who knows who wins on Oscar night? We do. We do."

166 SEASON 2, EPISODE 4 (1990): Bart caught a 3-eyed fish that was mutated by radiation leaked from Mr. Burn's nuclear plant. In 2011, a fisherman caught a similar 3-eyed fish near a nuclear power plant in Argentina.

167 SEASON 2, EPISODE 9 (1990): Marge organized a censorship campaign which resulted in pants being placed on Michelangelo's nude statue of David. In 2016, a replica of the statue was to be unveiled in Russia and residents voted to cover the statue or not. Some schools had banned the image.

168 SEASON 2, EPISODE 18 (1991): Ringo Starr appeared as himself and answered some very old fan mail. In real life, Paul McCartney learned about a tape fans made in 1963. The BBC was responsible for the find and Paul wrote back.

169 SEASON 3, EPISODE 4 (1992): Lisa predicted scores of Super Bowl 26 with a Washington Redskins win over the Buffalo Bills. Next Year, the same episode aired but changed 'Skins to Cowboys and the Cowboys beat the Bills in SB 27. The same teams met the following year, the same episode was aired and again accurately predicted a Cowboy win over Buffalo.

170 SEASON 3, EPISODE 24 (1992): In the episode, a machine was demonstrated that translated Maggie's baby-cries into English words. Such tech was non-existent at the time, but it is today. Companies like 'zoundream' fundamentally work and even look like the device pictured in the Simpsons.

171 SEASON 4, EPISODE 8 (1992): Homer eats too

much at an All-You-Can-Eat restaurant and he's thrown out. He sues the establishment. Five years later, a man sued an All-You-Can-Eat restaurant in Massachusetts because he was thrown out after 7 hours of eating.

172 SEASON 4, EPISODE 20 (1993): There is a tradition in Springfield where residents drove snakes to the center of town and "whacked" them to death. In 2013, residents of the Everglades started an annual event called "python removal." Cash awards are given to those participants who killed pythons humanely.

173 SEASON 4, EPISODE 21 (1993): This particular show has been proclaimed as maybe the best example of Simpsons "predictive programming" in one episode. A juicer is shipped from Osaka, Japan to Springfield. But before this, *two Asian packers sneeze germs into the box!* Springfield breaks out with an epidemic called the "Osaka Flu." This was 7 years before the CoronaVirus, which supposedly came from an eastern country. The citizens riot and demand a cure. Dr. Hibbert tells the crowd that all they need is "bedrest." The episode not only reflected the demand for a vaccine, but the social-distancing of staying at home. Bees were also attacking Springfield. China and Japan have a history of deaths from bees and hornets. In 2019, giant Asian hornets were found in the Vancouver area of North America.

174 SEASON 5, EPISODE 10 (1993): Mr. Burns opened a casino in Springfield and 'Gunther & Ernst' performed with their white tigers who attacked the men. Ten years later, a white Bengal tiger attacked Roy of Siegfried and Roy. Roy was partially paralyzed and the popular Vegas act suddenly ended.

175 SEASON 5, EPISODE 13 (1993): Homer uses a tiny camera in a large hat. Such hat-camera technology was not on

the market at the time. Years later, we find the same "head-cams" in a wide range of sporting events.

176 SEASON 5, EPISODE 15 (1993): NASA sends an average person into space and that person is Homer. In 2013, the UK held a contest for average people to be shot into space. A young man was chosen and launched into space.

177 SEASON 5, EPISODE 19 (1993): Doris the Lunch Lady added horse meat to the cafeteria's food, an illegal act. In 2012, UK health officials found very high levels of horse meat in a wide range of beef products.

178 SEASON 6, EPISODE 8 (1994): The Simpsons joked about Apple's 'Newton,' which was bad at recognizing hand-writing. This episode predicted auto-correct to hand devices.

179 SEASON 6, EPISODE 19 (1995): The episode was set in future-London and it showed an odd-shaped skyscraper along with Big Ben and the London Tower. But 14 years later, "The Shard" was erected as the tallest building in London. Not only is its shape similar to the drawn tower, but the *location in London was correct!*

180 SEASON 6, EPISODE 19 (1995): The episode was set in the future. Lisa's husband spoke into his watch and it was 20 years ahead of "smart watches" and picture-phones.

181 In the same episode, her and her husband's room in college had a Rolling Stones poster on the wall. It joked of the band's age with: "The Steel Wheelchair Tour 2010." But in 2010, the band was still going strong, performed for the President and played the Super Bowl halftime show in 2006.

182 SEASON 6, EPISODE 25 (1995): Mr. Burns blocked out the Sun! Twenty-eight years later, George Soros planned to block out the Sun over Antarctica in an effort to slow

its melting.

183 SEASON 9, EPISODE 1 (1997): The Simpsons go to NYC. Lisa holds up a booklet with a bus coupon that offers trips to New York City for "$9."

The coupon just so happens to have the Twin Towers right next to the $9 and that forms '911.' This is extremely significant and aired 4 years before September 11, 2001. The Simpsons went to NY and had a terrible experience.

184 SEASON 9, EPISODE 12 (1998): Bart is drawn to a video game called "Yardwork Simulator," an interactive CG game. Years later, video games are filled with situations similar to yardwork, but not at the time of the episode.

185 SEASON 9, EPISODE 25 (1998): This episode contained 'Up, Up and Buffet,' an airplane restaurant. Various airplanes have since been converted into restaurants.

186 SEASON 10, EPISODE 1 (1998): Homer and Bart steal grease for high profits. In 2008, high prices for oil "created a blackmarket for grease." Grease thefts occurred across the country. One man stole 300 gallons of grease from Burger King.

187 SEASON 10, EPISODE 2 (1998): Homer scribbled

on a blackboard and "almost, exactly" calculated the Higgs-Boson or "God Particle," which two scientists later won the Nobel Prize.

188 SEASON 10, EPISODE 5 (1998): A graphic on a news show read: "20th Century Fox, a division of Walt Disney Co." In 2019, Disney announced a giant merger with 20th Century Fox.

189 SEASON 10, EPISODE 22 (1999): Homer and physicist-genius Stephen Hawking drank together at Moe's Bar. Hawking agreed with Homer's idea that the universe was *donut-shaped.* Four years later, cosmologists found evidence that supported a universe that "curved and was empty in the middle."

190 SEASON 11, EPISODE 5 (1999): Homer splices together tomato seeds and tobacco seeds and creates the "tomacco" plant, a bad tasting fruit that's addictive. In 2003, Rob Baur grafted a tomato plant onto a tobacco plant and was successful in producing a fruit similar to the one on the Simpsons. This fact delighted the show's staff.

191 SEASON 13, EPISODE 22 (2002): Fat Tony glued cotton on ferrets and sold them as "designer dogs." In 2012, a man bought 2 toy poodles and discovered they were massive ferrets on steroids.

192 SEASON 15, EPISODE 8 (2004): The show had Moe supposedly closing down a Toys-R-Us store. This was 14 years before the chain of stores closed in 2018.

193 SEASON 16, EPISODE 8 (2005): In the Simpsons world, Canada had legalized marijuana. In the real world, Canada legalized pot in 2018.

194 SEASON 17, EPISODE 10 (2006): Homer is trapped in an underwater submersible vehicle and his oxygen runs out!

In 2023, OceanGate's 'Titan' went on a voyage to explore the wreck of the Titanic and the *craft imploded and killed 5 people onboard!*

195 SEASON 17, EPISODE 11 (2006): Viewers saw the future when Lisa was President of the U.S. She talked of the mess left by the last president: *Donald Trump!* In 2016, Donald Trump won the U.S. Presidential Election.

196 In the Simpsons movie (2007), the family escaped a huge dome that was put around Springfield. The NSA tracked them by their phones and through video surveillance. In 2013, Ed Snowden revealed that the real-life NSA had been doing the same thing for years.

197 Also, in the Simpsons movie, the government used Tom Hanks to pitch their agenda for the destruction of Springfield. In 2022, Tom Hanks appeared in a promotional video and put a positive spin on the Biden administration.

198 SEASON 18, EPISODE 3 (2007): The Simpsons family visit a shopping mall where they see a dilapidated and out-of-business JC Penney store. Fourteen years later, the store chain filed for bankruptcy.

199 SEASON 20, EPISODE 4 (2008): Homer voted for Obama, but the voting machine registered it for his opponent, John McCane. In real-life, voting machines were shown to be faulty when votes for Joe Biden went to Mitt Romney.

200 SEASON 20, EPISODE 4 (2008): A shocking hint of the future is displayed when Homer kills Prince in an elevator! Eight years later, the singer/songwriter was found dead at his Paisley Park home in Minnesota. He died, "accidentally overdosing on fentanyl." And he was discovered in his own personal elevator.

201 SEASON 21, EPISODE 12 (2010): Homer and

Marge compete in Curling in the Vancouver Olympics and won against the favorite, Sweden, in a big upset. Sweden is always favorites in Curling, but surprisingly lost to the U.S. in 2008.

202 SEASON 22, EPISODE 1 (2010): Martin, Milhouse and Lisa made a betting pool of who will win the Nobel Prize. In 2016, one of the names written on the pool actually won the Prize (Jaqdish Bhaqwati) for Economics.

203 SEASON 23, EPISODE 10 (2012): News items are seen at the bottom of the screen which read: "Europe puts Greece on Ebay." In 2015, the prediction very nearly came true: Greece bailed out of 3 major loans and almost lost the ability to use the Euro as a monetary exchange.

204 SEASON 23, EPISODE 22 (2012): Lady Ga-ga performed for the town of Springfield where she hovered over the people, suspended on wires. Five years later, Ga-ga's act for the Super Bowl halftime had her lowered to the stage on wires.

205 SEASON 25, EPISODE 15 (2014): The show depicted Richard Branson in space. In 2021, Richard Branson became the first billionaire to fly into space with his own spacecraft.

206 SEASON 25, EPISODE 16 (2014): Homer became a ref for international soccer and found corruption and bribery in the game. One year later, FIFA's headquarters were raided and top officials in international "football" were arrested for corruption and bribery.

207 SEASON 29, EPISODE 1 (2017): In an alternate, parallel universe [like the plots of a lot of recent movies], the Simpsons are a poor family from Medieval times. Homer revives a dragon and it flies over a nearby village. The creature rains fire down upon the town and destroys it! This is eerily close to two years later in 'Game of Thrones' when a dragon

was sent and destroyed Kings Landing.

FUTURAMA is owned by the Simpsons and produced by the same company.

208 In 'Lesser of Two Evils' from Futurama's second season, there is a literal Miss Universe Contest with contestants from other planets. The host names Lela as the winner, which was wrong. The flowers and tiara are immediately removed from Lela and given to the appropriate winner. This mirrored a real-life pageant in 2015 where host Steve Harvey named Miss Columbia the winner. This was a mistake and the actual winner was Miss Philippines. Miss Columbia was stripped of crown and sash and they were handed to the winner, same as the Futurama episode.

209 In a 1998 episode of Futurama, Professor Farnsworth invented the "Smell-O-Scope," which was designed to amplify smells. Twenty-four years later, the "Nasal Ranger" was created. It is a device that focuses and amplifies the smell of distant things.

Anagram 'Coincidences'?

210 **A Bacon, Lettuce and Tomato Sandwich** = dad wants to eat a nice combo at lunch.

211 **A Beautiful Mind** = I am fine, but duel. (as in the movie).

212 **Abraham Lincoln** = I'll ban a monarch.

213 **A Bridge Too Far** = RAF, brigade too.

214 **Academy of Motion Picture Arts and Sciences** = studs of cinema anticipated Oscar ceremony.

215 my nice Media coup: attend fine actors' Oscars.

216 **A Carton of Cigarettes** = I got a taste for cancer.

217 greatest of a narcotic!

218 **Across the Universe, the Beatles** = Let It Be's verse echoes thru NASA.

219 **A Farewell to Arms** = realms of war tale.

220 **Agatha Christie** = rich hag is at tea.

221 **Albert Einstein** = Elite Brains.net.

222 **Alcoholics Anonymous** = O my, no occasional lush.

223 **Alexandre Dumas** = a sex 'n duel drama. (The famous author wrote 'The Three Musketeers,' 'The Count of Monte Cristo' and 'The Man in the Iron Mask').

224 **Alice in Wonderland** = inane, new Caroll did.

225 drew in on dalliance.

226 wanna nice ol' riddle?

227 **Alice's Adventures in Wonderland** = enslaved in ascertained un-world.

228 **Alice's Adventures in Wonderland, the Old Fairy Tale** = a sure enchanter, ideal for Disneyland: Walt loved it!

229 **Alice in Wonderland, Tim Burton's Film** = on Lewis Carroll, in mine, but daft mind.

230 **All Quiet on the Western Front** = he'll question war-front tenet.

231 the silent, eloquent war-front.

232 **Alzheimers Disease** = haze is real mess, die.

233 **A McDonald's Burger** = real dog and crumbs.

234 **Amelie Mauresmo** = arouse me, I'm male. (former French tennis pro that appears masculine).

235 **America** = I'm a race.

236 **American Bandstand** = a mad cannabis trend.

237 **Americans** = are maniacs.

238 **America's Got Talent** = a lot great acts in me.

239 **Ammonium Nitrate** = ammunition, a term. [as in fertilizer-bomb?].

240 **Anabolic Steroids** = calibration dose.

241 lab's idiots-race, no?

242 **An Alcoholic Beverage** = gal, can I have cool beer?

243 **Andy Roddick** = dinky odd arc. (another former tennis pro).

244 **Andy Warhol** = draw only, ha.

245 **Animated Motion Pictures** = put cartoons in Media item.

246 a pet in its cartoon medium.

247 O, I print cat and mouse item.

248 **Anime Cartoons** = so not American.

249 **Anthony Hopkins** = phony skin hat on? (Anagram suggests the well-known scene in 'Silence of the Lambs').

250 **Apollo Landing Site** = spot in Galileo land.

251 **Apollo Thirteen** = an or little hope.

252 plot, or the alien?

253 a trip to one hell.

254 other alien plot.

255 or patient 'hello.'

256 **Apple Macintosh** = laptop machines.

257 **Arc of the Covenant** = contract of Heaven.

258 for Heaven contact.

259 **Area Fifty-One** = fear a tiny foe!

260 **Ariel Sharon** = Oh, ran Israel. (He did).

261 **Arnold Palmer** = man rolled par.

262 **Arnold Schwarzenegger** = he's grown large 'n crazed.

263 **Arthur Wellesley Wellington** = well, well, English Tory nature.

264 **Artificial Insemination** = I fail? Aim it in containers.

265 **A Shoplifter** = has to pilfer.

266 **A Signal of Distress** = it's S.O.S. read in flags.

267 **Astronomer** = Moon starer.

268 **A Tale of Two Cities by Charles Dickens** = i.e. Darnay's cell switch, to see back of it.

269 a head block is Carton's sweet felicity. (Dickens' classic story contained a Charles Darnay and a Sydney Carton! *Very specific).*

270 **Athletic Supporter** = the testicular prop.

271 **Atomic Bomb** = BOOM at ICBM.

272 **Australian Open** = one Li Na, a star up. (former pro).

273 **Away in a Manger, No Crib for a Bed, the Little lord Jesus, Lay Down his Sweet Head** = after a tired new mother's journey, a holy babe laid in swaddling clothes, awes.

274 **Axl Rose** = oral sex.

275 **Babe Ruth** = he rub bat.

276 **Barack Hussein Obama** = Arab back in USA

homes.

277 **Bartender** = render tab.

278 **Bartenders** = beer 'n darts.

279 **Bart Simpson** = imp's brat son.

280 **Beatles** = able set.

281 **Beauty Contest** = bony, cute teats.

282 cutey, not beast.

283 eye to scan butt.

284 **Bela Lugosi** = I'll go abuse.

285 **Betty Grable** = leg, Battery B. (She was a popular pin-up girl during WW2 ["Battery B"] and known for her curvy legs).

286 **Big Brother and the Holding Company Featuring Janis Joplin** = high in public, for they're prone to big ganja joint and LSD, man.

287 **Bill Gates** = glib Tesla?

288 **Billy the Kid** = killed by hit.

289 **Boa Constrictor** = I, cobra, contorts.

290 ribs contact, *orr.*

291 **Bob Marley** = bomb early. (Does the anagram hint of the singer's early death?).

292 **Boris Becker** = therein spin/lob by racketeer. (Former German tennis star was arrested for tax fraud in 2023 and spent 8 months in prison. His anagram shows his sport and may hint at the scandal).

293 **Boris Yeltsin** = riot sensibly.

294 **Bosnian War Crimes** = Serbian racism won.

295 **Boy George and Culture Club** = a once-cute, burly, old bugger.

296 **Brain Surgeon** = boring a nurse.

297 **Breasts** = bra sets.

298 **Breast Implants** = bra/tits: men's pal.

299 meant bra splits.

300 **Brian Wilson** = slow in brain. (Songwriter for the Beach Boys had bouts of depression and a nervous breakdown in the '60s, which left him with a mental condition).

301 **British Airways** = this is war by air.

302 is this wiry Arab?

303 **British Broadcasting Corporation** = horrid, patrician, bigot, snob actors.

304 dictator Birt's phobic on-air groans.

305 botching Birt's crap to air on radios.

306 oh no, a boring Birt radio-cast script.

307 bigot chat radio: no script or brains. These are stunning and prophetic anagrams, especially if you were British. Baron John Birt is a former "Director-General" of the BBC.

308 **British Realm** = bar Hitlerism?

309 **Bruce Springsteen** = bursting presence!

310 **Butch Cassidy and the Sundance Kid** = deducted U.S. city banks, cash in hand.

311 dudes snatch city cash, bunk and die.

312 **Camilla Parker Bowles** = Balmoral screw like pa. (Once paramour to now King Charles, her anagram just happens to mention a well-known, royal castle).

313 **Camilla Rosemary Parker-Bowles** = beware, a royal prick's more small.

314 I am a merry raw bollocks pleaser.

315 Balmoral pricks awesomely rare.

316 was arse-licker, am royal problem.

317 amiable porker screws amorally.

318 **Captain James Cook** = I am ocean's top Jack.

319 **Captain James T. Kirk** = maniac parks jet kit. (The vague anagram might suggest that Captain Kirk parks the Enterprise?)

320 **Captain John Smith and Pocahontas** = champs join hands to patch a nation. (As the story goes, the Indian chief's daughter saved the lives of Captain Smith and his men. Pocahontas was key in the establishment of peaceful relations in early Jamestown and she was honored on a U.S. Postage stamp).

321 **Chairman Mao** = I am on a march.

322 I am a monarch.

323 **Chariots of the Gods** = horseshit! Act of God!

324 **Charles Lutwidge Dodgson** = *as gold, seducing the world.* (How did Lewis Carroll, writer of 'Alice in Wonderland,' seduce the world?).

325 **Charles Lutwidge Dodgson, English Author and mathematician** = has got on him the magical drugs that Alice used in Wonderland.

326 **Charles Lutwidge Dodgson, Lewis Carroll, Author** = a girl called Alice through wondrous world sets.

327 **Charles Manson** = men can slash, or.

328 harm clean sons.

329 **Charlton Heston** = on the NRA's cloth. (The famous actor's anagram seems to imply his stance on Gun-Control).

330 **Chris Evert** = server itch.

331 **Chris Martin, the Coldplay Singer** = last CD? crap! I ignore lines, rhythm.

332 **Chris Martin and Gwyneth Paltrow Become Parents** = contact grim star, why? their newborn's named 'Apple.' (The famous couple truly named their son: Apple).

333 **Christian Fundamentalist** = truth? Fact is, man's in denial.

334 **Christianity** = chastity, INRI.

335 **Christmas tree** = search, set, trim.

336 **Christina Aguilera** = uglier, Satanic hair.

337 **Christopher Columbus** = such trip, such bloomer.

338 cool ship's rum butcher.

339 he is much corrupt slob.

340 robs much, cruel to ship.

341 **Christopher Reeve** = script: he ever hero.

342 thrive creep horse? (The actor's first anagram might tell of his role as Superman. The second one is very strange and may describe his horse accident that left him disabled).

343 **Chrysler Corporation** = oh, cornerily sport car.

344 lorry is crap, torch one.

345 The Lorry Scrap Iron Co.

346 **Church of Scientology** = goofy, rich-chosen cult.

347 rich con's goofy cult, eh?

348 **Cindy Lauper** = end up a lyric.

349 **Circumstantial Evidence** = can ruin detective's claim.

350 can ruin a selected victim.

351 **Clint Eastwood** = *Old West action.*

352 **Clint Eastwood, the Actor** = I do that cool Western act.

353 **Clint Eastwood, Film Producer** = mid flop, re-edit, cut! won Oscar.

354 **Close Encounters of the Third Kind** = cold feet or thin-skinned touchers.

355 host children ride ten-cent UFOs, OK?

356 **Coelacanth** = a lone catch. (A live Coelacanth was

caught in late 1938 at the mouth of the Chalumn River on the east coast of South Africa. The prehistoric fish was thought to be extinct. Captain Goosen and his crew had no idea of this important discovery at the time.

357 **Communications Satellite** = COMSAT: metallic, noise unit.

358 **Communist Manifesto** = not immune to fascism.

359 **Condoleeza Rice** = I concealed zero? *(Really?).*

360 led zero cocaine? *(Really?).*

361 **Conservatives** = craven Soviets.

362 **Conspiracy Theory** = hysteric crap, no? Oy.

363 **Courtney Love** = very cool tune.

364 **Cristiano Ronaldo, Manchester United** = so dance around team in Antichrist role.

365 **Danica Patrick** = car-captain kid.

366 I'd panic a track.

367 **Danica Sue Patrick** = pick a car and use it.

368 **Daniel Craig** = a girl can die.

369 **Daniel Day-Lewis, the Actor** = ideally, I wanted the Oscar.

370 **Daniel Gabriel Fahrenheit** = infrangible heat dial here.

371 I label heat here and in frig.

372 I label infra-red heating, eh?

373 **David Crosby, Solo, If I Could Only Remember My Name** = very dim fool, bald slob, cocaine's ruined my memory.

374 **David Crosby, Stephen Stills, Graham Nash, Neil Young** = hey man, boring old cunts sing shit verses all day, pah!

375 **David Letterman** = nerd amid late TV.

376 **Dean Martin and Jerry Lewis** = sad Italian 'n merry Jew nerd.

377 **Debit Card** = bad credit.

378 **Declaration of Independence** = no finer deed, an ideal concept.

379 fine peace intended, darn cool.

380 end colonied era if act penned.

381 in defiance, deprecate London.

382 **Declaration of Independence, The** = can pen a nice old deed of thirteen.

383 **Declaration of Independence, U.S.** = free land: nation seceded in coup.

384 **Depression** = person dies.

385 **Designated Driver** = danger is diverted.

386 **Diana Spencer** = <u>nice snap, dear</u>. (Anagrams for Princess Di printed here and later in this book point to the tragic events of her death).

387 Prince: a sedan.

388 inane car sped.

389 pain ends race.

390 **Diana Frances Spencer** = *ascend Paris,* en France.

391 a Press Dance in France.

392 **Dido (Florian Cloud de Bounevialle Armstrong)** = so artful individual bloomed, record: 'No Angel.' (Dido's album is called 'No Angel').

393 **Director of the CIA** = oh, fierce dictator.

394 **Dirty Old Man** = randy, I'm told.

395 **Donald Rumsfeld** = led old arms fund.

396 **Donald Rumsfeld, Defense Secretary** = condescended elder, rule Army staff.

397 **Donald Trump** = mad old PR nut.

398 **Dracula, Prince of Darkness** = snarl, sucker fancied a drop.

399 **Dr. Alois Alzheimer, the German Neurologist** = memories going, lost in a rather dull…er…haze.

400 **Duke Ellington** = liked long tune.

401 **Earth** = heart.

402 **Eddie Arcaro** = I adored race.

403 **Edgar Allan Poe** = large lane dope.

404 plan a large ode.

405 ape and all gore.

406 Lenore, a pal? Gad. (The anagrams reveal Poe's usage of opium and 'Murders in the Rue Morgue' by ape and even the lost 'Lenore').

407 **Einstein** = I intense.

408 **Election Results** = lies, let's recount.

409 **Elizabeth Taylor, Actress** = total rich star, eyes blaze.

410 **Elvis** = lives!

411 **Elvis Aaron Presley** = seen alive? Sorry, pal.

412 earns lovely praise.

413 lives on as replayer.

414 **Elvis Costello** = voice sells lot.

415 **Empire State Building** = I am entitled 'super big.'

416 **Enrico Fermi** = i.e. I'm for CERN!

417 **Federal Bureau of Investigation** = if found alive, abuse, interrogate.

418 favorite agent buried alien's UFO.

419 **Ferdinand Magellan** = men find a large land.

420 **Florence Nightingale** = reflecting on healing.

421 angel of the reclining.

422 lice, filth, gangrene, no?

423 fetch Nigel an iron leg.

424 leech front-line gang.

425 left Henri congealing.

426 fetching linen galore. (The many perfect anagrams for the woman who "started modern nursing" during the Crimean War are fantastic. They accurately portray this British organizer who cared for soldiers and the feel of a hospital for wounded soldiers).

427 **Florence Nightingale, Nurse** = heroine, curing fallen gents.

428 **Franklin Delano Roosevelt** = vote for Landon 'ere all sink.

429 love for Stalin, rankled one.

430 not a novel deal for real skin. (President FDR's anagrams are remarkable. They specifically mention his political opponent, Alf Landon, and Stalin and his proposed 'New Deal').

431 **Frodo Baggins** = bad ring's goof. (from Lord of the Rings).

432 **Funeral** = *real fun.*

433 **Galileo** = I all ego.

434 **Galileo Galilei, the Italian Physicist** = on a high Pisa, I elicit/tally legalities.

435 **Gandalf** = fag n' lad. (Ian McKellen is a known homosexual).

436 **General Custer** = curse Grant, Lee.

437 **George Bush** = he bugs Gore.

438 **George Walker Bush** = rake, who glubs beer.

439 **George Walker Bush, the President of the United States of America** = takes power after foe, Mr. Clinton, but gee, he's sure a shit-headed git.

440 Empire State ego: he is a genuine bastard. Fuck the rest of the world!

441 debate it less. We ensure a gung-ho dictatorship of the Free Market.

442 seek bin Laden. He set out after Osama, forget it, he screwed right up.

443 **George Washington** = war on, he gets going.

444 engaging to whores.

445 a gent goes whoring.

446 **Gillian Anderson** = alien's DNA on girl.

447 no aliens, darling.

448 aliens land on rig.

449 and aliens on girl.

450 long alien drains. (She played Scully on the X-Files).

451 **Gloria Steinem** = on girlie teams.

452 male, ignores it. (gay-rights activist).

453 **God Bless America** = I massacred globe.

454 slice 'em Arab dogs.

455 crises: geld Obama.

456 **Goethe** = the ego.

457 **Grateful Dead** = dreadful gate.

458 **Great Britain** = battering IRA.

459 **Greenhouse Effect** = huge trees offence.

460 **Gustave Eiffel** = gave us lift fee.

461 **Halley's Comet** = shall yet come.

462 **Harley Davidson Motorcycles** = very costly old road machines.

463 **Harry Potter and the Chamber of Secrets** = three chaps try to reach tomb, nerds fear.

464 **Harry Potter and the Goblet of Fire** = portray battle of frightened hero.

465 **Harry Potter and the Half-Blood Prince** = happy creator: enthrall, hot, forbidden.

466 **Harry Potter and the Order of the Phoenix** = hide an extra depth of rotten horror-hype.

467 **Harry Potter and the Philosopher's Stone** = horrid Snape threatens, hope, trophy lost.

468 **Harry Potter and the Sorcerer's Stone** = horrors enchant stereotypes' retard. (Did the anagrams come first?).

469 **Henry David Thoreau** = a very hidden author.

470 **Henry Kissinger** = King Henry lives!

471 **Hermione Granger** = renaming her Ogre.

472 **Hillary Roddam Clinton** = I'll anchor dirty old man.

473 **Hillary Rodham Clinton** = lynch harlot in mid-oral.

474 Monica, horny-thrill lad.

475 drill: halt horny Monica.

476 **Homer Simpson** = he romps in Mo's.

477 **House of the Rising Sun** = O sure, fine song, US hit.

478 **Houston,Tranquility Base Here, the Eagle has Landed** = er, oh hi, hello again: ended a lunar quest by the States.

479 **Human Resources** = secure man-hours.

480 **I Can't Get No Satisfaction** = 'cos a Stone can't fit in a git.

481 a fantastic song, notice it.

482 **International Space Station** = it is not a pleasant container.

483 O, CIA, antenna listens, patriot.

484 **It's Been a Hard Day's Night** = and hey, this band is great.

485 British set, handy agenda.

486 **It's Beginning to Feel A lot Like Christmas** = O big liar felt enchanting mistletoe kiss.

487 tell Santa: come in, bring those gifts I like.

488 **Ivanhoe by Sir Walter Scott** = a novel by a Scottish writer.

489 **James Bond** = M, send a job.

490 **James Cameron, Director** = set major cinema record.

491 **Jehovah's Witnesses** = the Jewish son saves.

492 **Jennifer Aniston** = fine in torn jeans.

493 **Jesus Christ** = such jest, sir.

494 JC thus rises.

495 **Jim Morrison** = Mr. Mojo Risin'. (Jim's only perfect anagram happens to be one of his song titles from the album 'LA Woman').

496 **Joe Biden** = I need job. (President Biden fated for the job?).

497 **Johannes Brahms, composer** = he's major Bach sponsor, man.

498 **Johann Sebastian Bach** = aha, enchantin' bass job.

499 **John Belushi** = lush on job, eh?

500 **John Elway** = he lawn joy.

501 **Johnny Cochran** = arch con Johnny.

502 **John Patrick McEnroe** = chronic top-name jerk.

503 no temper in arch jock?

504 **John, Paul, George and Ringo** = golden ganja, heroin group.

505 **Jonathan Frakes** = ha, Jon's a Trek fan. (STNG star).

506 **Jose Canseco** = Joe's con case. (The former pro

baseball player named several star players as steroid users in a 2005 book).

507 **JRR Tolkien's The Hobbit or There and Back Again** = hear, hear Bilbo at Bag-End! Join hot tricks 'n trek.

508 **Judas Iscariot, the Disciple** = I aid to epic lad: Jesus Christ.

509 **Judy Garland** = jug lady, darn.

510 **Justine Henin** = hi, June tennis.

511 **Justin Leonard** = led, just an iron.

512 **Justin Timberlake** = I'm a jerk, but listen.

513 **Kate Winslet** = wet tale, sink. (Star of the film: 'Titanic').

514 **Kurt Cobain** = croak in tub.

515 **Lebron Raymond James** = modern joy realms: NBA.

516 yes, male-born M. Jordan.

517 **Lee Harvey Oswald** = lay overhead, slew.

518 revealed: who slay.

519 lo, we've had slayer?

520 he was a lovely Red.

521 **Leni Riefenstahl** = senile Hitler fan. (She was a Nazi filmmaker for Hitler).

522 **Leonard Bernstein** = rare blend in notes.

523 **Leonard Nimoy** = I led Moon yarn.

524 **Leonardo Da Vinci's The Last Supper** = depict all persons and the Saviour.

525 ends: avid apostles repair to lunch.

526 Opus Dei Dan: Christ veal on plaster.

527 apostolic pleasure, had TV dinners.

528 **Leonardo Da Vinci, the Artist Genius** = Italian's hands receive tutor in God.

529 **Leonardo DiCaprio** = ocean idol or a drip. (*Titanic* star).

530 **Leper** = repel.

531 **Lev Nikolaevich Tolstoy** = O, it's a lovely thick novel.

532 **Listen** = silent.

533 **Lock, Stock and Two Smoking Barrels** = do let's clock Sting's barman work, OK? (This is a very specific one which reflects Sting's role in the film. Sting owned 'JD's Bar').

534 **Lord of the Rings** = Frodo, shire, LTNG.

535 **Lord of the Rings by John Ronald Reuel Tolkien, The** = thrilling nether-land journey of three old books.

536 **Lord of the Rings Trilogy, JRR Tolkien's** = torrid, gory, elf trek: thrills, join song!

537 **Lord of the Rings, the Fellowship of the Ring, Volume One, JRR Tolkien's, The** = help join trek West then South of Shire length. Frodo fell in River Gloom.

538 **Lord of the Rings, the Two Towers, The** = Frodo, the gentlest whore's is worth it.

539 **Lord of the Rings, the Return of the King** = frightened knights honour elf torture?

540 **Los Angeles** = Angels lose.

541 **Los Angeles Police Department** = dragnet people toss me in a cell.

542 crime agents: all stoned people.

543 **Lubrication** = oil act in rub.

544 **Lysergic Acid Diethylamide** = giddy, chemicalised reality.

545 **Madame Curie** = me, radium ace.

546 **Marc Bolan** = BLAM! No car. (Singer for the glam-rock band T-Rex died in a car crash, which his name implies.

Would the crash not have happened if he spelled his name 'Mark'?).

547 **Mark of the Vampire** = freak VIP to Hammer. (Hammer Films, known for its scary monsters and vampires).

548 **Marcello Mastroianni** = also romantic, manlier.

549 I'm also Latin romancer.

550 actor's realm in Milano.

551 **Maria Sharapova, Tennis Player** = am a pain as trophy rival, Serena?

552 **Marie Antoinette** = one in a trim-a-tete.

553 a termination tee.

554 terminate on a tie. (She was beheaded).

555 **Marilyn Monroe** = in lore, my Norma.

556 many minor role.

557 I marry loon men.

558 marry no oilmen.

559 **Marlene Dietrich** = nice Hitler dream.

560 I'd leer at rich men.

561 reel charm in edit.

562 cinema hit, Dr. Leer.

563 **Marquis de Sade** = queer, sad maids.

564 **Martina Navratilova** = variant rival to a man.

565 **Mary Kay Letourneau** = amour? Nay, a tyke lure.

566 **Mary Queen of Scots** = O fear my conquests.

567 **Mary Shelley's Frankenstein, or the Modern Prometheus** = here, he reanimated smelly trunk of shy monster person.

568 **Mary Wollstonecraft Shelley** = hey, tall fellow, scary monster!

569 **McDonald's Restaurant** = menu: cold rats and rats.

570 **Medal of Honor** = damn fool hero.

571 **Medicinal Marijuana** = a cure? I'm in a damn jail!

572 **Mein Kampf by Adolf Hitler** = OK, print my half-mad belief.

573 imply it baffled Herman, OK? (The anagram seems to refer to Nazi Hermann Goring).

574 **Mercury, Venus, the Earth, Mars, Jupiter, Saturn, Uranus, Neptune and Pluto** = just nine planets may arc up round the Sun, ah, pure art ever true must run.

575 nine planets turn around Sun: her rays put her temperature, just vacuum.

576 my, just vacuum true super-heater. Her part: nine planets turn around Sun.

577 **Merry Christmas and Happy New Year** = starry hype, many wrap merchandise.

578 **Michael Collins, the Astronaut** = it's Moon launches that I recall.

579 **Michael Jackson** = manacle his jock.

580 hijack calm nose.

581 he's jail cock man.

582 **Michael Richards** = held a rich racism.

583 hear racism, child? (Seinfeld's Kramer made a spectacle of himself with an act where he displayed *racism* against blacks).

584 **Michelle Obama, First Lady** = I + BHO created small family.

585 **Microsoft Windows XP** = worm downs PC, so fix it.

586 **Military Headquarters** = red alert: U.S. may hit Iraq.

587 **Missing Persons** = Spring Session M.

588 impress in songs.

589 sings on, impress. (Did the band *Missing Persons* know of their anagrams? 'Spring Session M' is the title of their first, break-out record album).

590 **Mona Lisa** = a man's oil.

591 **Mona Lisa, The** = ah, not a smile?

592 **Mona Lisa, Da Vinci's** = maid in oils, canvas.

593 **Mona Lisa, Leonardo Da Vinci's the** = Oh, her odd, Italian smile on canvas.

594 **Mona Lisa Gherardini Del Gioconda, The** = hanging art, I smile. Leonardo hid a code. (Da Vinci Code).

595 **Monica Lewinsky** = money was in lick.

596 cosily wank men.

597 my known CIA lies.

598 I knows I'm nice lay.

599 **Monica Samille Lewinsky** = Slick Willie's my A-one man.

600 **Monica Seles** = camel noises. (Former tennis star known for her very loud grunts).

601 **Montgomery Cliff** = comfortingly fem.

602 **Mother of Mercy** = my Comforter, eh?

603 **Mother-In-Law** = *woman Hitler!*

604 **Mount Saint Helens** = as hot eminent nuls.

605 **My Sweet Lord by the Former Beatle George Harrison** = GH regrettably a 'He's So Fine' melody/meter borrower. (A very specific and incredible anagram that refers to a famous lawsuit. In 2015, George Harrison was found guilty of "subconscious plagiarism" and had to pay $1,599,987 of his earnings from 'My Sweet Lord').

606 **Nancy Kerrigan** = grace 'n any rink.

607 **Napoleon Bonaparte** = no, not appear on Elba.

608 no, a trap open on Elba. (He ruled Elba for 300

days).

609 **National Aeronautics and Space Administration** = aim is to land pods in/near USA area. Can it? No, it can't.

610 **Nikola Tesla** = take all ions.

611 last alien, OK?

612 talk so alien.

613 alias: ol' Kent.

614 it a son: Kal-El. (Tesla created our modern world and received little credit for amazing things like AC Current, radio, TV, etc. He was called "the Man who Fell to Earth" and "SUPERMAN of the Industrial Age." There are many shocking anagrams that suggest that he was an alien and also references to the Superman story (the Kents and Kal-El).

615 **Nikola Tesla, the Inventor** = kilovolt antenna? it's here! (vague description of Tesla's wireless NY Power Tower).

616 **Nova Scotia and Prince Edward Island** = two Canadian Provinces, lands I dread.

617 **Nuclear Power Station** = a near core, lit-up towns.

618 **Oliver Twist by Charles Dickens** = wretched Victorian's Bill Sykes.

619 swarthier Bill Sykes convicted. (There are many stunning anagrams that reveal the plot of the story and repeatedly mention the 'Bill Sykes' character).

620 **Orenthal James Simpson** = OJ, he Seminal sportsman.

621 Heisman plot, snare Ms. OJ. (won the Heisman).

622 immense harlot, OJ snaps.

623 inept OJ slashes mom, ran.

624 Ms. OJ's Ron, lame thespian.

625 I'm OJ, slashes neat Ron, PM.

626 patrolmen hiss OJ's name.

627 jam, solemn Shapiro sent.

628 OJ's solemn, Marsha inept.

629 OJ, less mama, then prison. (What's in a name? If it's OJ's and certain other people's names, then there seems to be something unnatural going on? Mere letters or words should not determine one's fate. And yet, they seem to in numerous cases of celebrities. Certainly not a matter of *coincidence).*

630 **Orson Welles** = now role-less.

631 **Osama bin Laden** = a damn alien SOB.

632 is a banal demon.

633 old man in a base.

634 a bad, neon Islam.

635 bad as Lenin, Mao.

636 I, bad man on sale.

637 O, banal man dies. (*Nothing good? Coincidences??).*

638 **Palestine Liberation Organisation** = I go plot a riot in Israel, an insane bet.

639 **Palestine Liberation Organization** = Israel at a TNT blaze, I ignore opinion.

640 **Paramedic** = came rapid.

641 **Parliament** = rampant lie.

642 PM: a Ten liar.

643 **Patrick Rafter** = far, racket trip. (former Aussie tennis pro).

644 **Patrick Stewart** = a crap Trek twist.

645 act as Trek twirp.

646 **Patrick Stewart, The English Actor** = he's captain to Star Trek crew, light.

647 **Pixar Films** = fix lamp, sir. (Their logo).

648 **Plan Nine from Outer Space** = run poorest film, a penance.

649 one man's picture near flop.

650 **Pope John Paul, His Holiness** = hope in Polish plan, Oh Jesus!

651 **Postman** = no stamp.

652 **President Putin of Russia** = in future despair, stops in. (A hint of the Ukraine crisis in this anagram?).

653 **President of Russia, The Putin** = I punish deepest frustration.

654 **President Trump** = Mr. Putin's Red pet.

655 **Prince** = nice PR.

656 **Prince of Wales** = crown if asleep.

657 **Princess Di** = sic spin, *red!*

658 spins, cried.

659 **Princess Diana** = *ascend in Paris.*

660 dies in car, *snap!*

661 a car spin is end.

662 sad panic risen.

663 car, snap, die, sin.

664 pain as car's end.

665 car ends as pain.

666 end as car spin. (The anagrams that surround Princess Diana are truly unbelievable how they describe details of her tragic death in Paris, in a car, and not far from a Greek statue of Diana – *as if her death was planned, staged or fated?*).

667 **Produce** = crop due.

668 **Prostitution** = it in/out sport.

669 **Public Relations** = crap, built on lies.

670 **Raiders of the Lost Ark** = Ford, the real star is OK.

671 **Ramone Navarro** = ran over a Roman. (This early, silent movie actor played the original Ben-Hur. Some of the actor's anagrams refer to the famous chariot race in the movie).

672 **Rap Music** = up racism.

673 **Restaurant** = eat, rats run.

674 **Richard Branson** = baron's darn rich.

675 **River Phoenix** = X heroin Viper.

676 X-hero PR, vein.

677 O, rip vein, her X.

678 or hex in Viper.

679 prior vein hex.

680 rev, pix heroin.

681 I've X-heroin PR.

682 no hirer ex-VIP.

683 expire nor HIV.

684 Oh, expire in RV.

685 heroin vex, R.I.P. (Young actor, River Phoenix, died of a heroin overdose right outside of the Viper Club in Hollywood in 1993. This was after he was supposed to perform at the club with a band of his famous musician friends. There were more creepy anagrams that clearly indicated the horrible tragedy).

686 **Robert Louis Stevenson** = novelist's true bore, son.

687 **Romeo and Juliet** = mated junior, ole.

688 la mort d'une joie.

689 one jilted amour.

690 **Rome Wasn't Built in a Day** = but laid in two years, man.

691 but nor was Medina, Italy.

692 A.D. Italian town by Remus.

693 **Ronald Wilson Reagan** = no darlings, no ERA law.

694 a lone insane warlord.

695 so grand an Orwellian.

696 goal now: slander Iran.

697 **Rudolph Valentino** = uh, top lover in land.

698 **Saddam Hussein** = has nudes, maids.

699 hides, damns USA.

700 I had U.S. madness.

701 hissed: "damn USA!"

702 U.S. ends him, sad.

703 **Salman Rushdie** = read, shun Islam.

704 **Sean P. Diddy Combs** = NY's cops did me bad.

705 **Sean Puff Daddy Combs** = Duff CDs by a spade, mon.

706 **September Eleventh, Two Thousand and One** = Oh, let's never doubt that men need weapons.

707 thou heaven sent new blood-spattered men.

708 never the debate on Laden, he must stop now.

709 the latent war depends on Bush. Even me, too.

710 one top event, Bush's theorem: Laden wanted.

711 new top event: Bush sent Laden to me, Oh dear.

712 stop there, Taleban wound even the demons.

713 the penous event: both towers, Laden named.

714 two home-bound planes threatened events. {Wow}.

715 **Serena Williams** = smiles, a real win.

716 MAN-wise rallies.

717 a Marseilles win.

718 **Serena and Venus Williams** = US raven maids seen win all.

719 **Seven Eleven Incorporated** = open it and never ever close.

720 **Sgt. Peppers Lonely Hearts Club Band** = crap LP sung by the LSD-prone Beatles.

721 **Shakespeare** = seek a phrase.

722 **Shakespeare, the Immortal Bard of Avon** = Oh,

this remarkable man's a favored poet.

723 **Sharon Tate** = Satan to her.

724 **Sherlock Holmes** = smells crook, heh?

725 **Sherlock Holmes and Dr. Watson** = handle damn, worthless crooks.

726 **Son of Sam** = of masons?

727 **Space Shuttle Challenger** = *the ascent, gasp, cruel hell!*

728 **Spandex** = expands.

729 **Spice Girls** = Geri's clips. (Geri Halliwell's topless videos).

730 **Star Wars Episode One: The Phantom Menace** = space as entertainment? Whoops, dear me.

731 set prior to 'A New Hope,' same man ascendeth.

732 handsome Emperor's won apathetic Senate.

733 ashamed Portman, Neeson were so pathetic.

734 Neeson, a master showpiece, hated Portman. (specifics!).

735 **Stephen King** = *the King pens!*

736 **Steve Martin** = I'm star event.

737 **Stevie Wonder** = er, doesn't view.

738 **Tesla Coil** = oscillate.

739 **That's One Small Step for Man, One Giant Leap for Mankind** = famed Neil Armstrong on pleasant Moon path talks fine.

740 **The American Dream** = meet a dear, rich man.

741 **The American Revolution** = our achievement on trial.

742 much tea in one river, a lot.

743 elation: much tea on river.

744 O, arm each volunteer in it.

745 **The Artist Formerly Known as Prince** = tiny, short freak relents: "I'm crap now."

746 no-talent prick with mere fans, sorry.

747 **The Beatles: Paul McCartney, George Harrison, Ringo Starr and the late John Lennon** = re-arranges nicely, shall let them be a darn great group, then. No one on chart?

748 **The Cigarette and Tobacco Industry** = death by cancer, to distinct outrage.

749 **The Columbia Astronauts** = acute human loss at orbit.

750 brutal outcome hits NASA!

751 **The French Revolution** = over the Chunnel for it.

752 **The Detectives** = detect thieves.

753 **The Duke of Wellington** = O, fleet knight, won duel.

754 one doleful, wet knight.

755 would the King not flee?

756 **The Hiltons** = hint: hotels.

757 **The Hound of the Baskervilles, Sir Arthur Conan Doyle's** = ah, rather nosy Sherlock hunts bad evil fiend, routs, ole.

758 hurrah, I said, and truly one of the best Sherlock novels.

759 **The House of Representatives** = thou see there a nest of vipers!

760 **The Houses of Parliament** = top man here's a foul shite.

761 loonies far up the Thames.

762 'Is not Heath asleep?'

763 a fearless Pitt, Hume, Hoon.

764 PM's of a hostile nature, eh? (more specific anagrams).

765 **The Hunchback of Notre Dame, Written by Victor Hugo** = French book about totty-mad revenge within church.

766 **The Irish Republican Army** = relay much pain, re: British.

767 IRA? a prime, slithery bunch.

768 yep, I can harm British rule.

769 **The Itchy and Scratchy Show** = on which Rat scythed shy Cat.

770 **The Jefferson Administration** = framed this joint's Free Nation.

771 **The Leaning Tower of Pisa** = when Italian, get for pose.

772 I warn thee of giant slope.

773 a foreign head 'e tilts now.

774 a steep roof, angle within?

775 **The Life and Adventures of Nicholas Nickleby** = Dickens: naïve enter fanciful Dotheboys Hall.

776 fine tale, find thou a novel by Charles Dickens.

777 novel by Dickens: oh, ah, real fateful incidents.

778 **The Middle East** = smelt death, die!

779 **The Moon** = not home.

780 **The Murders in the Rue Morgue, by Edgar Allan Poe** = you remember, one ape hurt and slaughtered girl.

781 **The Mystery of Amelia Earhart** = aerial safety, that her memory?

782 **The NASA Mars Exploration Rover Mission** = O Roman planet has visitors or examiners.

783 O roams: horn proves alien Martians exist!

784 **The NASA Space Shuttle Discovery** = evades catastrophe in such style.

785 ecstasy to see launch pads thrive.

786 evade loss in trusty escape hatch.

787 spy cased the astronaut's vehicle.

788 **The National Weather Service Forecast** = chief event alert, wear those raincoats.

789 **The Nobel Prize for Literature** = a terrible one for the Pulitzer?

790 **The Nuclear Regulatory Commission** = your rules clone atomic nightmares!

791 **The Olsen Twins** = new tits n' holes?

792 **The Passion of Jesus Christ** = just the pain of his crosses.

793 **The President of Russia** = Putin, hardest foe, rises.

794 sheer disaster of Putin.

795 **The Prince of Wales** = I, who left a Spencer.

796 wife's place: throne?

797 if the Crown please.

798 Charles wife, no pet.

799 loath wife: Spencer.

800 flew in, cop the ears. (Prince of Wales then, is now King Charles).

801 **The Republic of Ireland** = flop Bertie Ahern lucid?

802 Bertie Ahern could flip.

803 free? Britain could help.

804 chief ale: Dublin Porter.

805 fear Dublin hotel price.

806 I retold Leprechaun fib.

807 Dublin PO: rifle act here.

808 land of epic Britain rule, eh? (As expected with these specific anagrams: Bertie Ahern is a former leader of Ireland).

809 **The Resurrection** = O Christ, U reenter.

810 torture enriches?

811 **The Reverend Charles Dodgson, Lewis Carroll** = Oh, he's clever: records Wonderland girl's tale.

812 **The Reverend Dodgson aka Lewis Carroll** = looks at girl, verses reached Wonderland.

813 **The Roland Garros Tournament in Paris, France** = R. Nadal, rather again, performs on tennis court. (Rafa Nadal won the French Open a record 14 times!).

814 **The Russian President** = Putin hears dissenter.

815 **The Salvation Army** = note vast Hail Mary.

816 O, hymn art's alive, ta.

817 or salivate at hymn.

818 They, I am Satan lover?

819 **The Satanic Bible** = isn't ethical, babe.

820 **The Satanic Verses** = scares the natives.

821 Christ! Nice ass, Eve.

822 **The Second World War** = chewed warlords, not.

823 **The Sign of the Cross** = he's right to confess.

824 **The Simpsons, a Cartoon** = a spot shot on Americans.

825 **The Simpsons Cartoons** = spastic Homer, snot son.

826 **The Sistine Chapel** = the speech is Latin.

827 it helps 'ace' the sin.

828 **The Sopranos** = a person shot.

829 shooters' nap.

830 **The Spanish Armada** = tar: "ships ahead, men."

831 meant as a hardship.

832 hardship at sea, man.

833 smash a pirate hand.

834 hard at ship, seaman.

835 am Death's piranhas.

836 **The Spirit of Saint Louis** = his feat is solo-unit trip.

837 his unit feat is solo trip.

838 hot plane is ours, is it fit?

839 **The Stanley Cup Final** = let fans hunt ice play.

840 **The Star Spangled Banner** = bars lend a pen strength.

841 grant a resplendent bash.

842 planted as brethren sang.

843 bands help arrange tents.

844 greatest land, brash Penn.

845 blest pennant has regard.

846 **The State of Israel** = foes are latest hit.

847 retaliates soft, eh?

848 **The State of the Union Address** = threats do not defeat Hussein.

849 **The Texas Chainsaw Massacre** = a man with axe chases actress.

850 **The Thirteen Original Colonies** = one coalition retireth English.

851 **The Three Stooges: Moe, Curly and Larry** = actors? Lord, they're an ugly threesome.

852 **The Towering Inferno** = enter hot wing on fire.

853 not worth fire engine.

854 **The United Kingdom** = O, dig the mud in Kent.

855 I didn't go nuke them.

856 O, it might end nuked.

857 knighted? I'm not due.

858 **The U.S. Library of Congress** = it's only for research bugs.

859 **Three's Company** = hepaysrent.com.

860 **Times Square, New York City** = it quite rocks my New Years.

861 **Titanic, The Sinking of the** = hitting of ice sank it then?

862 **To Boldly Go Where No Man Has Gone Before** = we ogle the gals onboard, be on form, honey.

863 ha, hero begs fellow to range beyond Moon.

864 **Tom Cruise** = I'm so cuter.

865 **Tom Selleck** = Stem Cell, OK. (The actor has publicly spoken about his skin treatments that involve stem cells).

866 **Tonya Harding** = grand hit on ya.

867 **Tony Blair, Prime Minister** = men, I'm Britain's Tory peril!

868 **Tree of Knowledge of Good and Evil** = God grew food in Eden, Eve took fall.

869 **TS Caladan** = *at scandal.* The author's unplanned anagram simply happened and was discovered later. Universal Serendipity~.

870 **TS Eliot** = toilets.

871 **Twenty Thousand Leagues Under the Sea** = huge water tale stuns, end had you tense.

872 **Union of Soviet Socialists Republic** = split is cause of countries' oblivion.

873 policies of revolution? Cuba insists.

874 fine politics to labour viciousness.

875 out-of-place Leninist obvious crisis.

876 boo Stalinist of precious inclusive.

877 boss Putin: civilize Aeroflot cousin.

878 Leninist faculties piscivorous.

879 Boris: sinful, vicious Police State, no?

880 O fie, boos evil Russian cunt politics.

881 split is cause of countries' oblivion.

882 basic uses of revolution in politics.

883 if politics abusive, censor solution.

884 so labour-intensive is politic focus.

885 October politicians' useful visions.

886 is previous ballot if conscientious.

887 politics of invasion, sluice out rebs.

888 labour councils poison festivities.

889 boo, it is up in collective of Russians.

890 Boris: sinful, vicious Police State, no? (Astounding! How can mere letters do that? Refer to Russian things and Russian people so specifically? Wait until you read anagrams for the United States).

891 **United States Air Force Academy** = academics; a fine, steady torture.

892 education? Read: 'Systematic Fear.'

893 U.S. cadet tries aerodynamic feat.

894 true aim? easy, cadets fornicated.

895 say, mate, rude cadets fornicate.

896 defend America, Russia yet to act.

897 **United States of America** = dine out, taste a Mac, fries.

898 face it, statue is no dream.

899 O France made its statue.

900 true ass, made Titanic foe.

901 constitutes a media fear.

902 tasted fierce Osama unit.

903 meat, fat, no rice: USA's diet.

904 fat roasted meat cuisine.

905 an armistice? to us, defeat.

906 eat our Fascist dementia.

907 a freedom at issue, intact.

908 M.I.T. a neat ace for studies.

909 atomic data use isn't free.

910 atomic tests are fun idea.

911 it can sue to deter Mafias.

912 I mandate a fist to secure.

913 a fate came to industries.

914 fears education at times.

915 Canada time, tourist fees.

916 O, neat crime data, use fist.

917 most cities feature an ad.

918 a farce, same destitution.

919 meet Arafat's seduction.

920 Sam: it's a cute Federation.

921 aim it at us, confederates.

922 I'm Castro-infatuated, see.

923 made treaties count, as if.

924 attain sauciest freedom.

925 I muse, fear not, taste acid.

926 if Democrats nauseate it.

927 dare set automatic fines

928 meet our fantastic ideas.

929 fantastic idea? Sure, to me.

930 duties Monica, eat faster.

931 Monica's diet, a true feast. (Truly shocking and unbelievable. Why do the titles of Russia and the U.S. refer to a vast number of things specific to their countries??).

932 **United States of America, The** = dine out feast, eat their Macs.

933 a tea fee started it, so much in.

934 ethnics? A fearsome attitude.

935 a neo-fascism attitude there.

936 it authenticates as freedom.

937 freedom's acute anti-atheist.

938 the dream: fine cause, toast it.

939 attitude there? O, a scam's fine.

940 their fates is to the educated man.

941 meta-truths in a sea of deceit.

942 I teach Freemasons' attitude.

943 a time, a fate, US to need Christ.

944 duties: teach man to eat fries.

945 the idea is fat cunts eat more.

946 I'm state-of-the-art audiences.

947 sent a comet Feratu: is death.

948 deceit, threat, animus of East.

949 Osama faced institute there.

950 ethnic Osama? Defeats it: true.

951 at true Defense, Osama hits it?

952 **Usain Bolt, the Sprinter** = O pal best runner, it's hit.

953 title is one sharp burst.

954 burst to the line. Sprain?

955 it able in the run-sports.

956 able in short petit runs.

957 this stable, top runner.

958 or I hit planet's best run.

959 **U Thant** = that U.N.

960 **Waco Stand-Off** = now of sad fact.

961 now scoff data.

962 was of daft con.

963 **Walt Disney's Winnie the Pooh**= went to slide his paw in honey.

964 **Walter Disney** = yields new art.

965 drew in a style.

966 **Walter Cronkite** = network recital.

967 network article.

968 **Walter Koenig** = low age in Trek.

969 **Washington at Valley Forge** = a few, they all go on starving.

970 **Weapons of Mass Destruction** = U.S. team swoops, finds no trace.

971 U.N. inspectors saw a doom-fest.

972 U.N. inspectors: doom? 'Twas safe.

973 atomic snoopers waste funds.

974 **William Jefferson Clinton** = in for fall, jilts nice woman?

975 jail Mrs. Clinton, felon wife.

976 **William Jefferson Clinton, President** = we'll join Monica L. in stiff red present.

977 **William Shakespeare** = we all make 'is phrase.

978 I'll make a wise phrase.

979 I am a weakish speller.

980 a wee phrase? I am skill!

981 **William Shakespeare's Antony and Cleopatra** = snake poisons were lethal act in a play drama.

982 **William Shatner** = slim alien wrath.

983 Will is Earthman.

984 hair sit well, man.

985 minstrel? Ha, wail!

986 **Wilt Chamberlain** = recall: I'm with NBA.

987 **Wimbledon Championships, The** = posh Tim Henman chips lob wide.

988 **Wimbledon Tennis Championship** = Tim Henman win possible? Do pinch!

989 **Wimbledon Tennis Championships** = I'm clownish

Henman: dippiest snob.

990 miss, do no spin/chip, Henman blew it!

991 **Wimbledon Tennis Championships, The** = bitch Henman lost, no? Whipped in semi.

992 Henman's time: he'd lob, chip, spin to win?

993 **Wimbledon Lawn Tennis Tournament, The** = new balls! Tim Henman to win? End not true. (Former British tennis pro Tim Henman never won Wimbledon).

994 **Wolfgang Amadeus Mozart** = a famous, German, waltz god.

995 gorgeous waltz, madam fan.

996 madman got far, *Zeus aglow!*

997 **Woody Allen** = wooed all NY.

998 **World Leaders** = Orwell's dread.

999 **The World Trade Center** = alert the tender crowd.

Can You Explain the Matrix?

No. Who can? Who can explain how life connects and moves and works as it does and why certain things happen as they do?

How did Nostradamus make all those predictions that came true? He may have used a device, a type of divining rod and *Ouija Board* or some other occult apparatus? It would make sense that the famous prognosticator from the 16th Century had a machine. A viewing-device where the future was displayed? Could the large amount of correct information from Nostradamus (not a matter of coincidence) have originated from a psychic source? Was the French astrologer/physician and seer one of the greatest psychics to have ever walked the Earth? Were aliens involved? We will probably never know how he did it until we build one of those Time-Screens, go back 500 years and *see* how he did it.

Let's explore a modern-day Nostradamus by the name of John Elfreth Watkins, Jr. We don't know much about him, not even the year he died. We know more about his father: John Watkins senior (1852-1903). He was Curator of Mechanical Technology at the U.S. National Museum (Smithsonian). He graduated from Lafayette College in 1871 and worked as a mining engineer. But in 1900, his son made *astounding predictions for the year 2000* and they were published in The Ladies' Home Journal. The predictions were not all completely true. The ones that were true are rather surprising. The father-son team of Elfreth Watkins begs the question: How was junior so accurate? Also, did the son's beliefs and predictions have anything to do with what his father worked on? Did he actually develop a kind of Time-Window and then pass along the information to his son? Time travelers? Does *time-traveling* explain how future things were known?

"Photographs will be telegraphed from any distance. If there be a battle in China a hundred years hence, snapshots of its most striking events will be published in the newspapers an hour later...photographs will reproduce all of nature's colours."

In 1900, such technical abilities were unheard of. It would have taken a week for a large event in China to have reached Western newspapers. The article did not explain how digital cameras or computers functioned, but the man clearly understood how COLOR pictures could be broadcast instantly over great distances. The only person that conceived of such things at the time would be Nikola Tesla.

"Americans will be taller by from one to two inches."

According to the BBC, Americans are generally two inches taller in 2000 than they were in 1900.

"Wireless telephone and telegraph circuits will span the world. A husband in the middle of the Atlantic will be able to converse with his wife sitting in her boudoir in Chicago. We will be able to telephone to China quite as readily as we now talk from New York to Brooklyn."

International phone calls did not exist in Watkins' time. Alexander Bell made the first call 15 years later and it was only coast to coast. A "wireless" telephone was a revolutionary concept.

"Ready-cooked meals will be bought from establishments similar to our bakeries of today."

Watkins was right about 'ready' to go meals in takeaway shops and in supermarkets.

"There will probably be from 350,000,000 to 500,000,000 people in America [the US]."

Watkins was off with this estimate; there were 280,000,000 people in the year 2000. Although, the prediction had it correct that the rate of growth would be less than the rate in the 19th Century.

"Winter will be turned into summer and night into day by the farmer with electric wires under the soil and large gardens under glass...Electric currents applied to the soil will make valuable plants grow larger and faster, and will kill troublesome weeds. Rays of coloured light will hasten the growth of many plants. Electricity applied to garden seeds will make them sprout and develop unusually early."

Greenhouses certainly existed in Watkins' time, but not the application of ELECTRICITY as a fundamental element in all phases of plant growth. It was not until 50 years later that electricity was used by growers, such as heating the soil and applied to seeds. Also, colored lights? Possibly, this is one innovation that has not been explored to the max?

"Man will see around the world. Persons and things of all kinds will be brought within focus of cameras connected electrically with screens at opposite ends of circuits, thousands of miles at a span."

Television! Actually an invention by Tesla (not Philo T. Farnsworth) was foreseen by John Watkins in 1900. Cameras and screens and images linked by electronic circuits at great distances? This only happened in the 20th Century and then later by webcams on the Internet.

"Physicians will be able to see and diagnose internal organs of a moving, living body by rays of invisible light."

A remarkable prediction of the Tesla-invented X-Ray Machine. Also, CAT-scans and ultrasonography are implied.

"Huge forts on wheels will dash across open spaces at the speed of express trains of today."

Tanks! Leonardo da Vinci designed such military vehicles and John Watkins expanded on the idea.

"Trains will run two miles a minute, normally. Express trains, one hundred and fifty miles per hour."

Exactly 100 years after these words were published, Amtrak's high-speed flagship called the "Acela Express" opened between Washington, DC and Boston. The Acela train is capable of reaching 150 mph.

"Strawberries as large as apples will be eaten by our great-great-grandchildren."

Fruits and vegetables have been enlarged these days and pumped up with artificial colors, flavors and nutrients that might not be safe to consume.

"All hurry traffic will be below or above ground when brought within city limits."

Fascinating, but not an accurate prediction. Many of Watkins' views were what should have been, not necessarily what will happen. *No cars in big cities!* If only~. The concept is not far from ideas presented at the 1939 World's Fair decades later, such as driverless cars and magnetic highways that made accidents impossible. Watkins correctly predicted elevated roads and subways.

"Everyone will walk 10 miles a day."

The idea appears as if it does not consider all the amazing means of transportation that will be developed in the years to come. Yet, Watkins emphasized exercise and activity, which is exactly what people should do.

"Mosquitoes, house-flies and roaches will have been exterminated."

Not correct, but they should be. Watkins, apparently, knew the wonders of Electricity and had far better knowledge of these things a hundred years before everyone else.

"There will be no 'C,' 'X' or 'Q' in our everyday alphabet. They will be abandoned because (they are) unnecessary."

I would have taken out the 'K,' but he's right. We don't need these letters and other letters could be substituted for them. Doesn't this hint of modern texting and abbreviating normal words? LOL.

We're left with a mystery of what happened to this guy and how'd he get these fanciful flights into Tomorrow? Did he peek into a parallel world that was close to ours? Something tells me that Mr. Watkins' guesses were not guesses. But your guess as to how this happened is as good as mine.

There are endless examples of how *forward-thinking* people were at the turn of the century. Not the last one, the one before that. Shocking "retro-future" artwork of flying suits, Free-Energy towers, wireless knowledge and technologies, instant communications, TV, atom bombs, satellites, antigravity, spaceships, moonbases, powerful Laser-weapons, moving sidewalks, jet-packs, medical cures, alien technologies, alien landscapes, and aliens, *way back in 1900!* The great Columbian Exposition of 1893 (Tesla lit) that offered a view of a fantastic future and included astounding feats in architecture. So much of humanity's imagination and dreams that did not happen. And some that have.

Who's to say there aren't real Time Machines and real Time Tunnels or vortexes that the Secret Government utilizes in Black Ops projects? We'll never hear about classified Stargates in the true sense, outside of fictionalized ones in the movies. Or what they have found on exoplanets? What if many of the aliens we know from TV and films actually exist? These would not be coincidences. You see, Hollywood writers and writers in general these days...have no imagination! Look at the dumb, insipid *schlock* that's been made into movies, especially over the last 10 years. Have we, our military, gone off-world and encountered real aliens? Yes. I'm sure that much of our stories have a solid basis in true events. Did some aliens visit Earth just before 1900 and demonstrate wonders beyond belief? Why not? It happened throughout the Old Testament.

Do the research yourself. See what has been imagined more than 100 years ago? The time of Jules Verne and H.G. Wells. Again, we do not know the full circumstances of how these projections came into existence during this era of Mega Creativity. Sure, everyone can dream of Things to Come. Occasionally, we'll be correct. But that is not what I'm talking about: I'm talking about the possibility of *extraordinary* means of discovering future events. Britain, and the governments under their control, are not going to inform you of what they actually have, what they really can do and what Reality is. "They" will "educate" you, inform you of everything that is not true and push/force you along wrong directions. THEY probably have advanced technology more than 100 years beyond the crap that they've given us little people, below the capstone. Like in the film 'They Live,' we're talking about the "power elite" and they don't *share*. Was the 2013 film 'Elysium' with Matt Damon true, in the sense: off-world, They have medical facilities and technologies far ahead of what we have down here on Earth?

I promised two more to make 1001 "COINCIDENCES." 1000 Pictured is a French drawing of what a classroom in the year 2000 might look like. Teaching appears to be an easy job. The schoolmaster simply feeds books into a machine and the machine instantly inputs the information into the heads of students. No, I don't think we (the people) have these types of devices, but so advanced for the time, eh? I wonder about this technology~.

I know Nikola Tesla thought of similar machines. Did you know he conceived and probably constructed a device that *Photographed Thoughts?!* <u>It's why we have television</u>. True.

According to a Kansas City Journal-Post front page in 1933, Tesla said that *thoughts leave an impression on one's retina* – from this discovery, a byproduct was developed and that was our television. They had TV decades before they decided to give it to us in the 1950s. (Tesla has the patent on radio, not Marconi).

Psychic mediums and crystal balls. There are honest to goodness, real telepaths and those with metaphysical abilities [X-Men]. And they usually work for the Government. One example may be Russian-born Nina Kulagina (1926-1990). She joined the Red Army at age 14, but she was a housewife during the time of her "alleged" powers. Old films of Nina demonstrated her *telekinesis* where she moved objects with her mind. One reason to believe the woman is that she was harshly condemned by Russian officials who went out of their way to discredit her again and again. Yet, Kulagina won a defamation suit against the Soviet government. Also, I remember her videos and she moved wooden matchsticks with her mind. It took a lot of energy out of her; I don't think it was an act. She was accused of using magnets. Magnets would not move wooden matchsticks.

Another example is Uri Geller. His bio reads:

"Uri Geller is an Israeli-British illusionist, magician, television personality, and self-proclaimed psychic. He is known for his trademark television performances of spoon-bending and other illusions. Geller uses conjuring tricks to simulate the effects of psychokinesis and telepathy."

The bio is hilarious because nothing is further from the truth. [This I know from a personal experience with the man where he spontaneously bent his hotel room key for me and a friend back in 1976. At the time, my psychic wife could do the same. I still keep a box of spoons/keys that I know were bent with the mind. One spoon was 100% untouched. If you'd have seen it bend completely in 30 seconds, you'd be a believer too]. So Wikipedia assumes there's no such thing as a telepath with extraordinary powers, eh? Don't tell that to Edgar Cayce. I guess Uri's just "conjuring" up voodoo BS and gullible people believe it? NO. Your government and the British government have used Uri Geller for his real abilities. The feud between Geller and the magicians has always been a concocted farce. Great Britain controls every side of opposing/situations they have created. Geller has been placed on airplanes, right next to known spies with confidential data burned on disks in their cases. Geller *fried* them with his *aura,* rendering them useless, under orders. Cold War, spy-stuff. The CIA was also very interested in receiving information by *remote-viewing* at the time. Stanford University tested Geller in 1973. Their conclusions were phenomenal and proved his abilities. They were most impressed how he could draw something that they had hid.

Back to the original idea: Are there methods to know the future before it happens? Absolutely, let me count the ways. By way of machines that produce time vortexes or "windows" into other time periods. Time Television. They can actually *go* into the past and future. Or, they can view it. Imagine what they can really do with technologies that they will not share with us<.

If one studies the events that surround *The Philadelphia Experiment,* you'll discover the late Al Bielek and his brother, Duncan. They were the ones who jumped off the USS Eldridge in October of 1943 *when they beamed the ship out of NY harbor* and everything went crazy! (The film was basically true). The story of Al Bielek and what happened later at Montauk NY is unbelievable, but real. I say "real" because Al was one of the smartest people on the planet and partially took over the federal Philadelphia project after Tesla left. He was one more genius used by the Forces That Be.

Investigators into Al Bielek's life will find that he and his brother JUMPED INTO THE FUTURE when they jumped off the ship! [Not in the movie]. <There are maps of great land changes Al saw in the future and reports of what those times were like>. Al also has been sent through time tunnels and dealt with aliens. Al's story is extremely unbelievable, yet realistic. Bielek worked with the large 2-legged Lizard creatures (known in Star Trek as the Gorn. They're real).

The following interview of Al Bielek comes from Brad and Sherry Steiger's great book 'The Philadelphia Experiment & Other UFO Conspiracies.' The Steigers were kind enough to grant permission to print quotes from the book and from Al Bielek:

"Duncan jumped overboard...and **went back to the future.** He was not there when the ship returned to its normal space/time. I was. And, I made a report…I told them Duncan and I had been to the future and all this and they (top brass) looked back at me with unbelieving stares...”

“...On deck (some) seemed to be insane; some babbled about ETs. I didn't believe it. I didn't believe it until I saw the paperwork from Oscar Schneider…up to that point, I had not seen an extraterrestrial or seen them on the ship…it all occurred after, after we jumped overboard…*the ETs came and went.*”

“In terms of 1943 time, it was about 4 HOURS (gone)…Elapsed time for the Eldridge being in hyperspace and time which Duncan and I spent in 1983, it was approximately 12 HOURS. Time is not linear; it can be BENT. (Al/Ed claims to have spent **6 weeks in 2137 and two years in 2749!)**…”

“Those guys were exposed to the magnetic fields for quite a long time and it was almost lethal. Today, we know this sort of thing. At the time, it was unknown. ONLY TESLA SUSPECTED IT and suspected quite correctly what the problems might be.”

“There were five others missing that also jumped overboard and disappeared. Why Duncan and I survived?…Our survival was arranged by someone for a purpose. The other guys were not supposed to jump…whoever was looking out for us was not looking out for them and *they evaporated.*”

“We both jumped and we could only see gray fog. That's when things got very strange. There was no water. We just kept falling, falling, falling…in a state of panic. We came out of this into a brightly lit area like open sky and a cloudy-effect, moving through the sensation like we were FLYING. Some higher Power was doing this for a reason, but we wound up in (the year) 2137!”

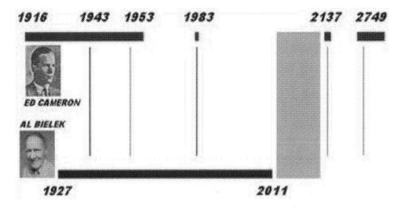

"He (Tesla) rejoined them in perhaps the late '30s because of his close connection with FDR...Tesla had been called to Washington to do work for the government. He was assigned to several projects, the principal one of which later resulted in the Philadelphia Experiment."

"One of Tesla's projects was the so-called '**Death Ray**.' Most people don't know this but the machine was actually built by the U.S. Army in 1938-'39 and was tested in New Mexico...the ray truly worked. It was so devastating and its effects so terrible that the *government decided that it was too dangerous for anyone to control. They destroyed the working model; they destroyed the records; they destroyed the plans.* The officers in charge said that they would rather see the thing destroyed than be put into possible use by an enemy...In 1940, Tesla proposed a similar system to the British, but in the form of a Particle Beam weapon system, actually an earlier development of his. He was also turned down by them."

"He (Tesla) became very concerned when he learned that the Experiment would now include a *live* crew. He protested that the scientists had no true idea of what would happen to the personnel onboard the ship. Everyone always talks about the genius of Tesla. Without taking any of his genius away from him, it must be admitted that *he was a very unusual person. I am convinced that he had a definite extraterrestrial connection.*"

"An acquaintance who used to work with Tesla has said that **he talked to 'someone' off-planet everyday.**"

"In March, 1942, all the levers were pulled to place the test ship, a battleship, into invisibility and nothing happened. I remain convinced that *Tesla sabotaged the Experiment*...there was no way that he would risk that many human lives...He left the Project, and ten months later, on January 7, 1943, he was found dead in his hotel room in New York." [Maybe not?].

"...But, instead of landing in the water of the Philadelphia harbor, we *landed in the grass at the Montauk Army Base on Long Island, New York! Dr. Von Neumann was waiting for us. It is said that he died in 1957. No way! He was there in Montauk in '83.*"

"We had somehow been sucked into hyperspace and been pulled into the future...Well, a UFO (craft) was sucked along with us to Montauk – and it was dismantled there!"

"The most important piece of equipment on the Eldridge was Tesla's 'ZERO TIME GENERATOR.' This incredible device was created to **lock into the basic Zero Time of our galaxy.** It provides a physical-cosmological lock-up that must be in place before one can attempt any exotic experiments in hyperspace..."

Al's (also Ed Cameron, it's very complicated) quotes sound far-out. Keep in mind that the Philadelphia Experiment involved the greatest minds at the time: Einstein, T. Townsend Brown, John von Neumann, Al Bielek and Tesla! If they could beam a destroyer and warp time/space more than 80 years ago, surely a simple thing like *seeing into the future* must be child's play today<>.

1001 For the last one numbered, check out this Colliers Magazine cover, May 1954. I have no way of knowing if this idea (and a million other wild leaps of imagination) was the result of "inside information" or strange coincidences? I'm betting publishers of magazines, creators of TV shows as well as filmmakers are Government agents, mostly. *They know~.*

Nikola Tesla would mention the old saying: "Everyone complains about the weather, but no one does anything about it." The great inventor actually did something about the weather. If you wanted to stop the rain, Electricity could clear the clouds away. If you wanted rain to change a desert into fertile lands, Electricity would provide the solution. Volcano eruptions or violent hurricanes could be terminated. With Tesla's World Wireless in place, he even planned to "illuminate the oceans." Why not? Unlimited power for everyone was possible in 1900! But, that did not happen. *We've been waiting for 124 years!* Maybe They are using his Electro-Magnetic Power Towers somewhere? But it's not on Earth.

Look at the Colliers cover again and see who wrote: 'Weather Made to Order.' Navy Captain H.T. Orville. He was, apparently, President Eisenhower's "weather wars" advisor. What are they not telling us? Maybe, also, mechanical ways to see into the future?

How could the Simpsons TV series have predicted so many things that have come true? Coincidence, or is something going on like *it's all connected at the top?* It is connected (also include Game of Thrones, the Super Bowl, the Olympics, the Oscars, etc.) along with other venues that most of the planet watches and is interested in. Some of the predictions have to be a matter of chance and it was pure guesses on the part of the Simpsons' writing staff. A few of the oddities must have happened all on their own without any collusion or conspiracy.

But why not place clues to the known future in popular TV shows, in movies, on album covers? Secret Societies get off on knowing things that you do not. How many times have guests come on the Johnny Carson Show and shook Johnny's hand in a secret handshake and we commoners at home never noticed? It is a covert Club on top and all of us poorer folk are on the bottom. If there were only a few of these odd coincidences, only a few Mandela Effects, only a couple weird Simpsons predictions and just a handful of Predictive-Anagrams and instances that made us scratch our heads and wonder WTF!! But there is an endless amount of strange items that just do not add up. Look closer at our world, study it at deeper levels, connect the patterns, feel inside...and the truth will be seen. ♀

 *A little inside information on the Simpsons. I actually worked on the Simpsons Show in its first 2 seasons, 1990 and 1991. [Yes, Doug Yurchey did]. Back when there was a "background clean-up" department, which is an obsolete department these days. No one thought the show would survive, even though it was a hit from the very beginning. Frank Zappa went around and shook everyone's hand. I saw Moon-Unit in the hall. Ah, those were the days. There certainly was not the slightest whisper of story-lines that were prophetic. This was a concept that brewed and exploded online 25 years later. Funny thing when you check the history of the Simpsons: It was first owned by a relatively small company in Hollywood. But after the first two very successful seasons, it was swallowed up by a larger company in North Hollywood. *That's suspicious to me;* why sell? Then big names like Conan O'Brien and others got more involved and the show skyrocketed worldwide. Close followers believe Season 5 and Season 6 were the best ("exceptional"). It's downright odd to me that Homer, Bart and the gang would be used by some of the top elites, who I believe have Time Mirrors and viewports into the future. Actually, it is not odd when you understand how the world really and truly functions. It's not how they tell you it functions. It might be that viewing other times ["Mirror, Mirror"] isn't a new technology, but an old one, and even an ancient one.

This book took one week to complete. I had already written a book called *The Anagramacron* and this volume contains some of the best anagrams. It did not take long to get out of me what had been boiling inside. I told the publisher this project would be titled: '1001 Coincidences?' At the time, I don't think I had one in mind. But I knew I could do it and did so in less than a week (99%). That means there are plenty more. Open your eyes, do some research work and I'm sure, in time, you'll understand what is going on and what has been going on.

Anagrams are simply LETTERS. Really? What's in a word? What's in a phrase? What's in a common expression? *Everything!* Anagrams are not simple puzzles or games we learned in school. Anagrams were honored, respected by kings and queens hundreds of years ago. Some kings had their anagramist right along with their royal astrologer. Spies and those participants in codes and espionage realized anagrams were perfect for their concealed messages, so they made anagrams that hid certain secrets. Lower classes formed anagrams that hid views against King and Country.

But, no...if you examine just the ones in the anagram section of this book [a micro amount of what is truly out there], it is a SHOCK! Mere letters should not do that! For example, either an early freemason created the title: "The House of Representatives" because they knew its anagram was: "Thou see there a nest of vipers,"...or...

The Universe did it! The serendipitous Matrix, the cosmos, aliens, God, WHOMEVER! Someone or something made these comments that are too closely attached to the subject of the anagram. Look at how many there are and the information given by them. Neutral letters (if nothing funky was going on) should spell out nonsense perfect-sentences and phrases. They would be abstract and have no relevance like, "Hand me the piano, fusebox." They certainly would not refer to the subject. But the PERFECT anagrams do! Perfect anagrams use every letter of the subject and form perfect sentences/phrases. Why do those perfect ones like Jim Morrison's: "Mr. Mojo Risin'" and Clint Eastwood's: "Old West Action" nearly always refer directly back to whatever was anagramed? They do and they shouldn't – what the hell?

What are the odds? But is the "Voice" of anagrams informing us of the pure truth? Yes, for the most part; see the great number of parallels in the perfect anagrams. Columns of anagrams that sure do relate to the anagrammed thing or person and found to be specifically accurate. Those are sentences and phrases that use every letter of the subject. *There really shouldn't be any perfect ones that relate, but they do!*

What the hell directs anagrams? Is it the same Spirit that moves a Ouija or manipulates Tarot Cards? Any connection to astrology? Possibly, in some cases, the anagram *Voice* is <u>not</u> revealing the absolute truth, but passing along the IDEA of news events or narratives of people and not the actual truth behind the scenes? For example, anagrams for the U.S. tell of a threat by "Osama," when Insiders know he was nothing more than a CIA "puppet" and was completely controlled, not the mastermind of 9/11. But anagrams did not inform us that 9/11 was an inside job. Another example is O.J. Simpson anagrams: They repeatedly imply he murdered "Ron" and his wife, "slash." But that story is for the public to consume. [O.J. didn't do it]. Ask Insider Dick Gregory and he will tell you O.J. was set up. But that idea is difficult to believe since Media minions pushed his *Guilt* so hard (under orders). Anagrams are not the pure truth in some cases.

Another possibility is a war between good angels and bad angels or Dark Spirits and Spirits of the Light? Poltergeist? Or aliens? Maybe they use or move such devices as pendulums, Ouija Boards, Tarot cards, crystals, etc.? And if you open a portal or a doorway [seen in movies] to, say, a positive dimension with good entities – don't you also open a means for negative forces to enter?

One side of our brain knows that letters of the alphabet should not conspire and have a *Voice* when they're just letters, like numbers. They shouldn't speak with personal opinions and even have an attitude. So we refuse to believe a weird paranormal phenomenon is going on. But the other side of our brain SEES the connections, knows the implications and kinda *blows a fuse* on the matter. How do we merge the two?

Is it a computer MATRIX? Are we in a simulation? Is that a valid and credible explanation to a lot of the mysteries? They have recently informed us through movies and paid shills on the Internet that we must be in an *artificial simulation,* like inside a holodeck on the USS Enterprise? What if they're right and we are in a simulation? The concept makes a little sense because...do you have the vision to see how bad it is out there, in the "real world"? Or are all the people who remember the Old World dead? You know, how it used to be? Things were supposed to get better in the future or in the 21st Century. Computers, robots were supposed to serve people and everything would evolve and improve. Is the society today better than it was a decade ago?? No. ***Everything has changed***

darkly, negatively. Haven't you noticed? It wasn't always fake, filled with gray people with gray cars and colorless souls, today's Walking Dead. Decades ago, people were colorful; *they were alive!* They had compassion and they cared much more than the youth of today, generally speaking. What happened? Change happened. But it wasn't a natural change. It seems like it was a mechanical change, a cold and heartless change as if our Human Overseers were tired of us and left? Are we in the hands of cold-blooded MACHINES? Machines, the things that were thought to help people, might just be in place now to hurt humanity and keep us *controlled?*

Possibly, when a black hole formed right off the bow of the USS Eldridge in 1943 and [real photo, note the mist pulled in] swallowed the ship...it was similar to our situation today? Could we have been pulled into a parallel reality about 10 years ago? That's when people around the world first noticed that the maps have slightly changed – lines in classic movies had altered just a bit – lyrics in a few songs were different – product names and logos were suddenly a tad different. Little things all over the planet had been slightly changed. It's been called the 'Mandela Effect' (I wrote 2 books about the phenomenon). The last thing you should do is believe what THEY say about it, in other words: its definition. What are the alterations, really? They are where this new Reality differs from the one that was here, from the one we were born into. The new Reality does not match the old one perfectly at every point: Here, here and over there, it differs. Plenty of people have remembered and noticed. But most of you guys walk through life *blinded* with your eyes open (Jordan Maxwell said) and have not noticed.

I've written 4 books about the dangers and threat this world is facing due to the A.I. that is firmly planted in every bit of our lives today. Look around you. It is truly everywhere now. "See what A.I. can do for your business." The 4 books are entitled: 'Artificial *Intelligense,*' 'Teran Tales,' 'Another Tera' and 'Tera,' where the A.I. has operated behind the scenes and runs every facet of Teran lives.

How could *they* have literally turned our world into its dark opposite? And people into their negative counterparts? Does the Mirror Universe that every main Star Trek series showed us have something to do with this? This world that is now negatively-charged? They knew? Was that one more damn coincidence with positive Trek characters who now explored their Dark Sides? Maybe they have done the dirty deed of planet-inversion through CERN? Doesn't that make sense? "We need more power, Captain!" CERN and possibly its build-up of negatively-charged energy reached a *tipping-point* and swallowed all of Earth in the same way the Eldridge was engulfed by a mini-black hole!? Just a theory.

If these lines of thinking were true, then, WHY? The answer might be for even more control over billions of us slaves. If we're in a computer simulation, then THEY have their hands on the controls and can fiddle with us any way they choose. They may be able to tweak our world with subtle changes that we would hardly notice these days. I'll give you a few examples:

There was always Jiffy Peanut Butter. It was called "Jiffy," according to many/many people. Suddenly it never existed? After the "massive Re-Set," reality altered and Jiffy became JIF. We were thrust into a world where that brand was always JIF? Yes. *But it has changed again.* Today's version is "Jiff," not all caps. But it was all caps not too long ago. *This is crazy.* These are not examples of announced product-changes. Reality has *changed,* meaning something extraordinary was responsible.

Another example is the ancient, golden mask of King Tut. We've seen it; it has been displayed around the world. Nothing should have changed it, but something changed it and then *changed it again.* Out of Tut's forehead protruded a snake or an asp. That's it. Then, when the Re-Set occurred around 10 years ago, suddenly a BIRD stood next to the snake! Two things now extended from the Boy-King's forehead. The bird was a full bird that stood there, from head to feet, next to the snake. Tut and Jiffy are only a couple of Mandela Effects where this Matrix or "new skin" that's been placed over everything is different from what it was, from what some of us remember. But the Tut mask has changed again, recently! Now the standing bird is not a standing bird: it is another serpent with a vulture's head! Two snakes? What? Yes! Someone or something is fucking with our reality and these so-called "Woke" people haven't even noticed. Forget Weather Wars, how about **Reality Wars**? What the hell is going on? Are we to expect even more subtle morphs of our universe and will they happen? When and what? What's going to stop them when they have all the power?

Kings and Queens do not share power, knowledge or technology.

The only answer for a better tomorrow, a good world for our children and our children's children, is out of our hands. On this point, I agree with J.M. It's too late; people are way too far gone and helpless and nothing is getting any better. The only hope for my people and my planet is Outside Intervention. How about a giant Mothership in our skies one day driven by positive aliens (angels) who do not want to eat us, but sincerely want to help us? True Space Brothers? Lovely space creatures only out to assist us, insure our growth and maturity. Good Teachers who will guide us to do the right things. If that scenario really happened, and the aliens were 100% legitimate and they were really going to drastically improve conditions for billions of people on the planet...

There would be a War of Worlds! The aliens would be attacked with all the nukes and might of Earth's combined military forces! Along with the First Strike, a Media campaign blitz would occur that demeaned the aliens and gave "credible" reasons for our attack against them. Our leaders would never allow outside help that changed their totalitarian State, their world Monarchy of Money-Enslavement. I wonder what would happen if they landed?

In movies, aliens land all the time. It used to be that some *fictional* aliens were peaceful. The first Star Trek series contained a number of peaceful aliens on higher levels, ("Above us like we are above the amoeba"). Such as the Organians, the Metrones, the Kelvans, the Talosians, the Vulcans, the Vians, etc. It's strange that the writers for that first series were credited sci-fi novelists, some of the best, such as: Richard Matheson (wrote maybe the best Twilight Zone episodes), Robert Bloch, Harlan Ellison, Jerome Bixby, Theodore Sturgeon. Something is odd here because in the mid-sixties, television sci-fi had no respect; there was no serious science-fiction on TV before Star Trek. *Voyage to the Bottom of the Sea, Lost in Space,* etc. Televised sci-fi was considered on the order of 'Captain Midnight' and 'Captain Video.' Trek was not tested and did have a few silly episodes. Why would famous novelists put their names on a project doomed to fail? They wouldn't. Unless the ST-narrative, as we've been told, is totally not what happened. It never had a chance for failure; it would return in a different form, year after year and decade after decade. All planned in advance, folks.

'Mirror, Mirror' is the prophetic Star Trek episode that first showed us the negative universe on the other side of the Mirror. Not a coincidence. Who understood at the time that this was exactly what every citizen of Earth will be pushed and forced into many years later? *They knew;* we were unaware. We're now all living inside a Star Trek episode, believe it or not~. Funny, the ST title was taken from Disney's 'Snow White and the Seven Dwarfs' animated feature film (1937). We all remember the Queen who asked her mirror: "Mirror, mirror, on the wall, who's the fairest one of all?" Well, presto, chango, some *Magic* of the universe has changed the classic line! The Queen now says, "Magic Mirror on the wall, who is the fairest one of all?" See the animated film and you'll see it begins with a storybook that opens. You'll read and hear these new words: "Magic Mirror." But we know and remember it was, "Mirror, Mirror." Why did the Star Trek title of that episode not change? It remains *Mirror, Mirror* ("residue")...exactly like most of us remember. Very odd, to say the least. If you examine the examples of Mandela Effects openly, many of them will ring bells, and you will realize they are not "mistaken memories." Someone or something is playing with us.

Star Trek Next Generation was a different thing entirely. No well-known writers of the sci-fi genre were involved. STNG was written by an in-house staff of writers. Notice, no more amazing extraterrestrials that operated on higher states of the mind. They consolidated that concept into one entity called the "Q." He wasn't cool. What a coincidence that the idea is the same one that is pushed in movies again and again: "There are no good aliens coming to your rescue, there are only bad ones that want to probe you, then eat you." I think STNG had a heads-up and the stories were contoured to meet a planned shape – or moved into certain directions that pleased the Hollywood Magician controllers [British Engineers]. Look at the 'Orville' series: *Pure Agenda.*

Help. We need help from good teachers that care.

We, the people, the children, should not have caretakers that are Machines or caretakers without hearts and souls. We should not be guided by mechanical men and mechanical women with mechanical hearts. We'll never be truly free until the People have Power. Real, flesh and blood people. Power to the People! When is that ever going to happen? When will the truth be recognized and realized and valued? When will the Darkness of Lies be seen and understood and be repulsed by the youth? Not embraced. When will we be truly *empowered* and know the difference between right and wrong?

I was a pen-pal with Nikola Tesla's son, Arthur H. Matthews. No kidding. I even talked to him once on the telephone. Arthur left this plane of existence in 1986. He co-wrote a book with Tesla called 'The Wall of Light' [the

Forcefield] that was printed by Health Research. Venusians met him on a number of visitations on his property in Canada. History does not record that Tesla had a son or was married, yet Arthur was his son ('Return of the Dove' by Margaret Storm). I'll never forget the *inside information* that Arthur revealed in hand-written postcards: 1) **"Tesla was always friends with JP Morgan"** and JP never pulled his funds from the NY Wardenclyffe Project. And 2) **"Tesla married in 1890, he had a son and died a rich man**." I believe Arthur, and I do not believe much of the stories the Media has created around Nikola Tesla. In Arthur's book, he compares the birth of Tesla with the birth of Jesus Christ. What if? What if JC had already come back to us? Does that explain Tesla's super-genius? JC, the Scientist? He brought Light to the world, and Electricity. Maybe he was so sick of the fucking Second World War that he left our planet in 1943?

On the phone, I asked Arthur, "When will we have Tesla's wireless power, Tesla Technology?"

He replied, "It will be so long in the future that no one then would have ever heard of Tesla."

We've waited so long and we're going to have to wait a bit longer. Humans are still military-minded. We're not going to have the Technology of the Gods (or Atlantis) until we are wise enough to use it properly.

NOT TOLD TO REMOVE THE TOWER,
TESLA REMOVED IT AT HIS OWN COST,
BECAUSE IT WAS THOUGHT IT COULD BE
USED AGAINST THE U.S. 2. BY THE
GERMAN'S. BY ALL MEANS DO NOT
GET INFORMATION FROM BOOKS. GET
TRUE FACTS FROM TESLA LECTURES, —
ARTICLES, PATENTS, AND HIS OWN LIFE
STORY IN "THE WALL OF LIGHT" — THIS IS
THE ONLY TRUE STORY!

Yours, Truly

Arthur Matthews

P.S. TESLA WAS A WISE MAN. NO ONE
CHEATED HIM. SOME DID TRY. HE GOT A
MILLION CASH FROM WESTINGHOUSE. IN 1893 —
IT WAS INVESTED, SO THINK IT OVER.
ALSO, TESLA SOLD ALL OF HIS PATENTS.
HE DIED HAPPY, AND RICH, DON'T BELIEVE WRITERS OF
ODD BOOKS.

INFORMATION IS FROM
THE PATENTS — LECTURES
ARTICLES, AND HIS
OWN LIFE STORY —
AND THE ONLY PLACE TO
FIND HIS LIFE STORY
IS IN "THE WALL OF
LIGHT" +
TESLA WAS NEVER A
DREAMER, ... HE WAS A
REAL MAN. HE BELIEVED
IN GOD — AND THE BIBLE,
HE MARRIED IN 1890 — HE
HAD A SON, AND HE DIED
A VERY RICH MAN.
SINCERELY

Arthur Matthews

GOD BLESS YOU
REAL GOOD FOR 1983
AND ALLWAYS!

JOY TO THE WORLD

TS Caladan

TS Caladan

Doug was born the only son of Rose and Steve Yurchey in Bridgeville, PA. in 1951. A loner, he drew pictures and dreamed of big/bright fantasy-worlds that were inside the comic book adventures he cherished. Movies, TV, stories, art, thrilled the young man, especially sci-fi and anything that had to do with aliens and life on other planets. He grew up interested in sports and earned a half-scholarship in tennis to Edinboro. After college, his interests turned to astronomy and various mysteries.

An unexpected event occurred: In 1973, he fell in love with a psychic who channeled. A 4-year marriage and a 'virtual Close Encounter' later, the young man was motivated to discover the truth in everything<. Odd occurrences happened during a strange marriage where spoons and keys bent with the powers of the mind. They met mentalist Uri Geller at this time. Wife Katrina did similar telepathic feats and their closest friends witnessed extraordinary things. In 1977, the marriage ended.

Doug moved to LA in 1982. He worked on the Simpsons Show in 1990-1991 as a background "Clean-Up" artist. After 2000, he became a prolific writer with many online articles, radio interviews and YouTubes of his work on Atlantis, Nikola Tesla and the World Grid. He was on 'Coast-to-Coast with George Noory' radio show and gave "the best interview since John Lear." Doug was filmed by National Geographic filmmaker Diego D'Innocenzo because of his theories on the ancient, rust-less, Iron Pillar in New Delhi. Nine million Italians saw the production on a TV Science show called 'Voyager,' with special-effects. His writing dreams came true and he was published by TWB Press in 2015. Now *TS Caladan,* the author's interests are Modern Mysteries and conspiracies or secrets behind Hollywood and the Illuminati. Then he discovered the Mandela Effect in 2019, which *changed everything~*. Tray Caladan is a mystery himself. He has spent more than 50 years of pure, honest, scientific research and today uses artwork and wild/far-out, sci-fi stories to deliver his conclusions and positive messages...*and, still, no one believes him.* [A few do].

Contact information for Tray Samuel Caladan:

tscaladan@gmail.com

Questions and comments are very welcome. Readers will receive quick replies. Thank you very much.

~tsc

Books written by TS Caladan (DH Jetson):

1) The Continuum
2) Son of Zog
3) The Cydonian War
4), 5) Science-Faction [Vol. 1 & 2], short stories
6) ANAGRAMACRON
7) inspiration
8) 2099, Transia~
9) The New Men and the New World
10) Beyond Barronsland
11) Mandela Effect
12) Best of TS Caladan
13) Mandela Effect II
14) Collected Comedy of TS Caladan
15) TS Caladan's Comedy II
16) Pez Wars
17) The PEZ-Effect
18) Ceana
19) PEZ 4 Ever
20) My Cat Book
21) Artificial *Intelligense*
22) Teran Tales
23) Another Tera
24) Tera
25) 1001 Coincidences

https://www.twbpress.com
Science Fiction – Supernatural – Horror – Thriller
and more